SURVIVING YOUR PRESCHOOLER

... A Mother's Manual

365 Activities for Two- to Five-Year-Olds
Using Mostly Things You Have At Home

Patricia Kuffner

Lighthouse Books
1992

Lighthouse Books
1423 Dayton Street
Coquitlam, B.C. Canada
V3P 1B3

Cover design by Kelly Brooks

First printing, December, 1992
Second printing, April, 1993
Third printing, December, 1993
Fourth printing, September, 1995

CANADIAN CATALOGUING IN PUBLICATION DATA

Kuffner, Patricia, 1960-
      Surviving your preschooler-- a mother's manual

      Includes bibliographical references and index.

ISBN 0-9696626-0-2

1. Education, Preschool--Activity programs.
2. Creative activities and seat work.
I. Title.

LB1140.35.C74K83 1992   649'.5   C92-091855-7

PRINTED IN CANADA

Table of Contents

Acknowledgements

There are many people who have contributed to this book, both directly and indirectly, and I would like to express my thanks to them.

First and foremost I acknowledge with love and gratitude my parents, Jack and Irene McGeorge, who have believed in me and supported me in everything I have ever done or wanted to do. They have given me many things: a love for the Lord Jesus; a belief in myself; and a determination to never say "It's good enough".

Thank you also to my dear husband Wayne, and children Andria, Emily and Joshua, who have put up with me this past year while I spent so much time "playing on my computer".

I am also very grateful to my sister, Carol Hannah, for her invaluable editorial assistance, to my brother-in-law, Jim Young, for his illustrating skills, and to my good friend, Bonnie Moody, for her helpful advice and comments. Thank you also to Dawn Steinke and the staff at Port Moody Pentecostal Tabernacle for generously allowing me access to their computer equipment.

To the rest of my family and friends who have encouraged and supported me throughout this project, I thank you all. I truly could not have done it without you.

For Wayne, my greatest gift,
and the three little arrows in our quiver,
Andria, Emily and Joshua.
(Psalm 127:3-5)

Introduction

"Each of us weeps--at least inside--when a child begins first grade, not because of the child we are losing, but because of the chances we've lost. So much is left undone."
Marguerite Kelly and Elia Parsons

The idea for this book came about one exceptionally rainy West Coast winter. Andria, my oldest daughter, was three. Her sister Emily was almost two, and baby Joshua was not yet six months old. Emily was in the midst of toilet training, and Josh nursed at least every two hours. Day after day we saw nothing but rain, and my normally sweet-tempered and easy-to-please three-year-old seemed to become increasingly moody and hard to deal with. I immediately signed up for a parenting course, somehow sure that I was lacking the necessary skills to deal with her.

What I ultimately discovered was that poor Andria was just plain bored. Although I knew I couldn't always expect to drop everything to get involved with her, I felt there was something I could do to provide her with a more creative and stimulating environment. I knew there must be activities that would both challenge and entertain. I wanted ideas for little projects we could work on together, but I also wanted things she could do on her own while I was busy elsewhere. Since we were living on one income, I also needed activities that made use of basic items we already had around the house.

Surviving Your Preschooler ... A Mother's Manual is the result of my desire to stimulate my own children. It contains ideas and activities for every situation and occasion, for both indoors and out, for summer and winter, for the quiet times and the rowdy ones. I have called this book *"A Mother's Manual"* mainly because it is a result of the fact that as a mother, I was at home, all day, every day, with three very young children (hence the *"Surviving"* portion of the title!). But be assured that this book is well-suited for anyone who has a preschooler in their life, be it mothers or fathers, grandparents, aunts or uncles, babysitters, daycare workers, preschool teachers, church workers or playgroup leaders. If you are looking for one good book on what to do with a preschooler and how to do it, this book is indeed for you.

Another note on the title of this book; it is called a *manual,* the definition of which is "a book easily held in the hand, especially one giving information or instructions" (*Random House Webster's College Dictionary*, 1991). This book is designed to be *used;* it is oversized for ease of handling, with large margins and lots of "white space" for your own notes and comments. It should be spattered with paint, sticky with paste, and smudged with fingerprints; well-worn after hours and hours of use. If this book sits on your shelf it will not be doing its job.

The activities in this book are suitable for children between the ages of two and five. Because there is such a difference in the abilities of children in that age range, some ideas will be too advanced for a two-year-old, and some will be too simple for a four- or five-year-old. Use your own judgement in choosing activities that best meet the capabilities and interests of your own child, and be prepared to supervise when necessary.

A note on the use of "his" and "her"; in recognition of the fact that children do indeed come in both genders, and in order not to show preference for either, the use of the male and female pronouns will alternate with each chapter.

I invite your comments along with any ideas of your own for activities or games that your children particularly enjoy. Please write to me at Lighthouse Books, 1423 Dayton Street, Coquitlam, B.C., Canada, V3P 1B3.

> *"It will be gone before you know it. The fingerprints on the wall appear higher and higher. Then suddenly they disappear."*
>
> Dorothy Evslin

Enjoy your preschooler! Don't let these precious years slip away; don't wait until kindergarten to realize the chances you have lost. My hope is that both you and your child will have many happy hours of playing, growing and learning together.

Patricia Kuffner
October, 1992

1.

Help! I Have a Preschooler!

"To be a good housewife and mother, you have to be more self-generated. You have to create your own playground of the imagination, and the mind. To be a really good, creative mother you have to be an extraordinary woman. You have to keep yourself involved with your child during great periods of the day when it's just the two of you and you feel that at any moment you may literally go out of your mind."

Meryl Streep

Preschoolers! They don't emerge overnight, or on your child's third birthday. It may happen so slowly you hardly notice it at all, but one day you realize that your clumsy, confusing little toddler is gone, and in her place is an easygoing, adventurous, energetic little child. While life with a preschooler can be a celebration, there will always be those days where it seems more like a chore. Your child may be a wonderful little person most of the time, but her boundless energy and relatively short attention span will no doubt result in some irritating, demanding and temperamental behaviour. But don't despair; chances are that she's just plain bored.

There are many ways to provide stimulation to your child. Often at around the age of three, children enter a preschool or playgroup for two or more days a week. A group such as this will usually provide your child with new friends and a new outlet for her creativity and energy. If your child is at home with you or another caregiver for all of every day, she relies on you to provide her with new experiences, outings and creative activities. Her day needs some structure, a loose schedule with recognizable breaks. She needs to meet people of different ages, adults and children alike. She relies on you to introduce her to books and music, art and craft projects, rambunctious games, and quiet learning activities. A short walk or some outdoor play should be part of every day.

While a variety of experiences and activities are essential to your child's development, resist the urge to push her too hard. All children need lots of time for creative and spontaneous play. Rather than assuming the role of teacher, instructing and directing your child, try to act as her helper in the learning process. Children need to learn on their own, whether it be in creative play or some of the more academic areas. They really need to run their own show, and know that you are there to help them when and if they need it. Children who have learned to direct their own play, who have been given lots of time to be creative and use their imagination, are less likely to experience boredom than those whose time is rigidly planned for them.

"BUT THERE'S NOTHING TO DO..."

All children, no matter how creative, imaginative and self-sufficient, will at one time or another experience a case of boredom or restlessness. Here are some suggestions to help you alleviate boredom in your preschooler.

Keep a Baker's Box in the kitchen.

A lot of your work time is probably spent in the kitchen, and your child will naturally want to be with you. Kitchen cupboards and drawers are full of interesting things that may prove irresistable to your child. Why not provide your child with her very own Baker's Box? Put together a collection of unbreakable kitchen tools for your child in a plastic crate or small storage box. Store it in a spare cupboard that is low enough for your child to reach on her own. She can use her tools for play, or when doing some cooking or baking with you. Some suggestions for a Baker's Box are:

- plastic measuring cups
- measuring spoons
- wooden spoon
- rubber spatula
- large metal bowl
- cookie sheet
- cake pan
- muffin tin
- pie plate
- cake rack
- cookie cutters

Have a Busy Box handy.

If you have a spare cupboard in your kitchen that is low enough for your child to reach, this is an ideal spot for her very own Busy Box. Take a small storage box or plastic crate and fill it with things that she can do on her own, any time she wants to. Good things to keep in a Busy Box are:
- crayons
- paper
- colouring books
- tape
- stickers
- scissors
- glue
- construction paper
- playdough
- cookie cutters
- ink pad with ink stamps

Make a Job Jar for your child.

Make a job jar for your child out of an empty jar, coffee can or small box. Cut strips of paper and on each one print a small job that needs to be done, i.e straighten your book shelves, wash the bathroom sink, put away the towels, wash the vegetables, pick up the toys, etc. You will know the jobs your child is capable of. While you do your morning chores, have your child pick a job from the job jar. The excitement of choosing her own job will probably take away her normal reluctance to work.

Take along a Busy Bag.

Be prepared for those times when you just have to wait ... at the doctor's office, at the hairdresser's, or in a restaurant. Turn a drawstring bag or backpack into a take-along Busy Bag that can be filled with special things to keep your child amused. Some suggestions for a Busy Bag are:
- crayons, markers, colouring books and paper
- stickers and a sticker book
- dolls and associated clothing, blankets, bottles, etc.
- matchbox cars
- puzzles
- ingredients for an *Edible Necklace* (see Chapter 5); shoestring licorice and cereal or crackers with holes in the middle
- magnets and a small metal cake pan (see *Magnet Fun,* Chapter 5)
- a special snack

Use your imagination. Make it a surprise, or have your child help you fill the bag before you go.

Rotate your child's toys.

Expensive store-bought toys are nice, but your child will lose interest in even the most creative toys when they are always around. By rotating her toys every four to six weeks, they will seem new to her and will be interesting and exciting all over again. To begin toy rotation, separate your child's toys into piles (if your child has a favourite toy, keep it out all the time). Keep one pile in your child's play area, and pack the others away in boxes, marking on them the dates they are to be brought out. This system will also work well for your child's books.

Make a Crazy Can.

Don't expect to come up with a new and wonderful idea off the top of your head when your preschooler starts driving you crazy. Make a list of on-the-spot activities that require no special materials, need no time-consuming preparation or clean-up, and above all, demand a minimal amount of adult participation or supervision. Write down these ideas on index cards or small pieces of paper and place them inside an empty coffee can. (If you like, cover the can with cheerful contact paper, or glue on plain paper and have your child decorate it with paints, markers or crayons.) When things start to get crazy (or when there's just "nothing to do"), choose a card from the can for an instant remedy. Appendix A on page 149 offers a suggested list of activities appropriate for your Crazy Can.

Look for new activities and experiences.

While children need free time for creative play, they also rely on you to introduce them to new projects, activities and adventures. This is hard to do on the spur of the moment, so some advance planning on your part is required. Try to schedule one or two different fun, challenging and creative activities each day. Decide on the activities ahead of time and have all the necessary supplies assembled in advance. Read on for some additional advice on planning activities for your child.

PLANNING YOUR ACTIVITIES

Failing to plan is planning to fail. Recognize the importance of planning new and creative activities for your child. You can have a shelf full of books on activities for children, or just this one, but the ideas this book contains are only valuable to you and your child if you use them (and if you don't do a little advance planning, chances are that you won't). Here are some helpful steps for planning your activities.

1. Read through *Surviving Your Preschooler ... A Mother's Manual* and fill in a weekly planner with activities you would like to try for each day. You can use a copy of the Weekly Activity Planner on page 7 or use your own calendar. Include a few alternate activities for when the weather won't cooperate or when things are just not right for what you have planned.

2. Using your weekly activity plan, make a list of supplies you will need and assemble or purchase them beforehand.

3. Make a list of what you need to prepare before your child becomes involved in the activity, i.e. mix paint, draw a treasure hunt map, etc.

4. If your child will be spending time with a babysitter, plan special activities for them and have all the necessary materials handy. This will let your sitter know that a day or night of TV watching is not an option.

5. Make a list of ideas that would be fun to do anytime you can fit them into your schedule. Have this list ready when you have some unexpected free time.

STOCKING YOUR CRAFT CUPBOARD

Whether you have a cupboard to spare, or just a box in the basement somewhere, here are some items you should have on hand for the various activities described in this book.

Things to have on hand:

aluminum foil .. aluminum pie plates (various sizes) .. bottle caps .. boxes .. brown paper bags .. buttons .. candles .. cardboard .. catalogues .. cereal boxes .. chopsticks .. clothespins .. coffee cans with lids .. coins .. confetti .. corks .. cotton balls .. cotton batting .. cotton swabs .. dried beans .. dried pasta (different shapes and sizes) .. egg cartons .. egg shells .. empty jars and lids .. envelopes .. fabric scraps .. felt .. greeting cards (used) .. junk mail .. lids from plastic gallon jugs .. magazines .. old clothes and costume jewellery for dress-up .. old mittens, socks, gloves for puppets .. old toothbrushes .. paint sample chips .. paper clips .. paper muffin cup liners .. paper plates/cups/bowls .. paper scraps .. paper towel/toilet paper tubes .. photographs of friends and family .. pine cones .. plastic bowls, lids, bottles .. playing cards .. popcorn .. popsicle sticks .. ribbon .. rice (uncooked) .. rubber bands .. ruler .. sandpaper .. shoelaces .. sponges .. spray bottle .. stickers from record clubs, etc. .. string .. styrofoam trays .. swizzle sticks .. thread .. thread spools .. toothpicks .. wood scraps .. wrapping paper scraps .. yarn scraps

Things to buy:

art smock (or an old shirt) .. beads .. chalk .. construction paper in various colours .. craft magnets .. crayons .. crepe paper .. glitter .. glue or gluesticks .. google eyes .. hole puncher .. masking tape .. newsprint (local newspaper or moving company) .. paper clips .. paper fasteners .. pencil crayons .. pencil sharpener .. pencils .. pens .. pipe cleaners .. plain writing pads .. ruler .. scissors .. self-adhesive paper .. stapler .. stickers .. straws .. tempera paints and brushes .. tissue paper .. transparent tape .. washable markers

WHAT ABOUT TELEVISION?

While some parents choose to alleviate boredom in their children by allowing them unlimited and unsupervised access to the family television, on the whole you should try to avoid using the television as an entertainer or babysitter. Although there are some innocent and educational shows available for young children, most of what children view on television is far from innocent and can be very detrimental to their emotional, intellectual and spiritual well-being. Children who spend a lot of time watching television can come to expect the instant stimulation that a fast-paced show can bring, and may be less likely to use their own imagination and creativity to stimulate themselves.

In his best-selling children's story, *Charlie and the Chocolate Factory*, author Roald Dahl wrote a wonderful little rhyme about television and the effect it can have on young children. He warns that while television may keep children occupied, we must take the time to consider exactly what it is doing to our young ones. He points out, with considerable humour, that it ..

" .. CLOGS AND CLUTTERS UP THE MIND!
IT MAKES A CHILD SO DULL AND BLIND."
"HIS POWERS OF THINKING RUST AND FREEZE!
HE CANNOT THINK -- HE ONLY SEES!"

Weekly Activity Planner

Week of:	To Do	To Buy
Sunday		
Monday		
Tuesday		
Wednesday		
Thursday		
Friday		
Saturday		
Rainy Day Options		

When parents in Dahl's rhyme contemplate, with not a little apprehension, how to entertain their children without a television set, he asks them to remember what children used to do before "this monster was invented":

"THEY...USED...TO...READ! They'd READ and READ,
 AND READ and READ, and then proceed
To READ some more. Great Scott! Gadzooks!
One half their lives was reading books!"

(Reprinted from *Charlie and the Chocolate Factory* by Roald Dahl, Alfred A. Knopf, Inc., New York, 1964, 145-147. Reprinted by permission of the publisher.)

You *can* use the television in a positive way by limiting your child's viewing to certain programs or certain times of the day. Watch the programs with your child and discuss what you have seen. Another alternative to negative television programming is commercially produced video tapes; look for tapes which instruct, entertain, and reinforce the values and principles you wish to develop in your child.

A WORD OF ENCOURAGEMENT

"*Motherhood brings as much joy as ever, but it still brings boredom, exhaustion, and sorrow too. Nothing else will ever make you as happy or as sad, as proud or as tired, for nothing is quite as hard as helping a person develop his own individuality--especially while you struggle to keep your own.*"

Marguerite Kelly and Elia Parsons

Be encouraged as you weather the stormy seas of parenting. Raising a preschooler is a monumental task which brings with it a great amount of work, but an even greater amount of joy. By providing your child with daily activities that are simple and fun, you are helping to make many happy memories of childhood.

2.

Basic Craft Recipes

"There is so much to teach, and the time goes so fast."
Erma Bombeck

Even at a very young age, your child can begin to develop his own creative skills and understand the artistic work of others. Visual art is not limited to paper and paint, but includes many different media. The craft materials in this chapter are essential for every child's artwork: paint, glue, paste, modelling compounds and more.

PAINT

Each of the following recipes will produce a good paint for your child to work with. Each varies in the ingredients required and the method used, so choose one that best suits the supplies you have on hand and the time you have available.

When mixing paint, keep in mind the age of the artist; as a general rule, the younger the artist, the thicker the paint (and brushes) should be. Paint should be stored covered; small plastic spill-proof paint containers are available at your local art supply store. These will hold brushes upright nicely without tipping, come with an air-tight lid for storage, and at several dollars each are well worth the purchase price.

Flour-Based Poster Paint

1/4 cup flour
1 cup water
3 Tbsp. powdered tempera paint
2 Tbsp. water
1/2 tsp. liquid starch or liquid detergent (optional)

Measure flour into a saucepan. Slowly add 1 cup water to make the paste smooth. Heat, stirring constantly, until mixture begins to thicken. Cool. Measure 1/4 cup of the flour paste into small jars or plastic containers. Add 3 Tbsp. powdered tempera paint and 2 Tbsp. water for each colour. For a more opaque finish, add liquid starch. For a glossier finish, add liquid detergent. Store covered.

Detergent Poster Paint

1 Tbsp. clear liquid detergent
2 tsp. powdered tempera paint

For each colour, mix together liquid detergent and powdered tempera paint. This makes enough for one painting session.

Poster Paint Extender

1/4 cup liquid starch
1/4 cup liquid detergent
1 cup liquid tempera paint

Mix together and add enough water for desired consistency.

Condensed Milk Paint

1 cup condensed milk
Food colouring

Mix a cup of condensed milk with drops of food colouring to make a very glossy, brightly coloured paint.

Cake Frosting Paint

Despite the enticing name, this is not an edible paint. It provides a thick frosting-like paint that your child can smooth and swirl into a design.

1 cup powdered tempera paint
2 Tbsp. wallpaper paste
1/4 to 1/2 cup liquid laundry starch

Mix powdered tempera paint with wallpaper paste. Add liquid laundry starch, mixing until the paint is thick enough to spread like frosting. Place the paint on a piece of cardboard and use a popsicle stick to make a design.

Homemade Face Paint

This face paint is suitable for painting designs with a small brush.

1 tsp. corn starch
1/2 tsp. water
1/2 tsp. cold cream
Food colouring

Stir together the corn starch and cold cream until well-blended. Add water and stir. Add food colouring, one drop at a time until you get the desired colour. Paint designs on face with a small paintbrush; remove with soap and water. Store in covered plastic containers or baby food jars.

Halloween Face Paint

This face paint is suitable for applying over a larger area, such as an entire face.

1 Tbsp. solid shortening
2 Tbsp. cornstarch
Food colouring

Mix shortening and cornstarch together until smooth. Add food colouring, one drop at a time until you get the desired colour. Use a sponge or your fingers to apply paint over a large area such as an entire face. To paint a design with a small brush, thin with a little water first. Remove with soap and water. Store in baby food jars or covered plastic containers.

Egg Yolk Paint

This recipe is suitable for use when painting edible cookies.

    1 egg yolk
    1/4 tsp. water
    Food colouring

Mix one egg yolk with 1/4 teaspoon water and lots of food colouring. Use a paint brush to paint on freshly baked cookies; return cookies to oven until egg has solidified.

FINGERPAINT

Each of the following recipes produces a good fingerpaint, however the ingredients and mixing method vary. Choose one that is suitable for the ingredients you have on hand and the time you have available.

Liquid Starch Fingerpaint

    1/4 cup liquid laundry starch
    2 drops food colouring or 1 tsp. powdered tempera paint

Your child can make up this fast and adequate fingerpaint himself. Mix the ingredients together in a small plastic bowl or cup.

Cornstarch Fingerpaint

    3 Tbsp. sugar
    1/2 cup cornstarch
    2 cups cold water
    Food colouring
    Soap flakes or liquid dishwashing detergent

Mix sugar and cornstarch together in a medium saucepan over low heat. Add cold water and continue stirring until the mixture is thick. Remove from heat. Divide the mixture up into four or five portions, spooning them into sections of a muffin tin or small cups. Add a drop or two of food colouring and a pinch of soap flakes or a drop of detergent to each portion. Use a different colour for each cup. Stir and let cool. Store covered in an airtight container.

Flour Fingerpaint

1 cup flour
2 Tbsp. salt
1-1/4 cups hot water
1-1/2 cups cold water
Food colouring or tempera paint

Put flour and salt in a saucepan. Add cold water and beat with a whisk or rotary beater until smooth. Add hot water and boil until mixture is thick. Beat again until smooth. Keep in refrigerator and colour as needed with food colouring or powdered paint.

Laundry Starch Fingerpaint

1 cup lump laundry starch dissolved in cold water
1 quart boiling water
1 cup pure white soap flakes or powder
Poster paint, water crayons or food colouring

Add the boiling water to the starch and cold water mixture and boil until thick. Remove from heat and stir in the soap. Divide into small containers and add colours as desired.

PLAYDOUGH

Everyone seems to have their own favourite playdough recipe, and many old favourites have been included here. Some require cooking, some are no-cook, some are meant to be eaten, and some are not. Choose the recipe that best suits your requirements and the ingredients you have on hand. Store playdough in a covered container or plastic bag. If it sweats a little, just add more flour.

Oatmeal Playdough

1 part flour
1 part water
2 parts oatmeal

Mix ingredients together well and knead until smooth. This is not an edible playdough, but will not hurt kids if they eat it.

Uncooked Playdough

1 cup cold water
1 cup salt
2 tsp. vegetable oil
3 cups flour
2 Tbsp. cornstarch
Tempera paint or food colouring

Mix the water, salt, oil and enough tempera paint to make a bright colour.
Gradually work flour and cornstarch in until the consistency of bread dough.

Peanut Butter Playdough

18 oz. peanut butter
6 Tbsp. honey
Non-fat dry milk or milk plus flour
Optional: cocoa or carob for chocolate flavor

Mix all ingredients together, adding enough dry milk or milk plus flour to
give dough the right consistency. Shape, decorate with other edible treats, and
eat!

Salt Playdough

1 cup salt
1 cup water
1/2 cup flour

Mix together and cook over medium heat. Remove from heat when mixture
is thick and rubbery. As the mixture cools, knead enough flour in to make
dough workable.

Coloured Playdough

1 cup flour
1 Tbsp. vegetable oil
1 cup water
1/2 cup salt
2 tsp. cream of tartar
Food colouring

Mix all ingredients together and heat, stirring constantly, until ball forms. Knead until smooth.

Koolaid Playdough

1/2 cup salt
2 cups water
2 Tbsp. salad oil
2 cups sifted flour
2 Tbsp. alum (available at your grocery or drugstore)
Koolaid for colour (or use food colouring or tempera powder)

Boil the salt in the water until salt is dissolved. Add food colouring, tempera powder or Koolaid for colour. Add salad oil, flour and alum. Knead or process until smooth. This dough will last two months or longer.

CLAY

Use the following recipes to produce a clay which can be rolled or shaped into ornaments. The drying methods vary, either overnight or in the oven. When hard, ornaments can be painted and preserved with acrylic.

Modelling Clay

2 cups salt
2/3 cups water
1 cup cornstarch
1/2 cup cold water

Stir salt and water over heat 4-5 minutes. Remove from heat; add cornstarch and 1/2 cup cold water. Stir until smooth; return to heat and cook until thick. Store in a plastic bag.

Bread Clay

6 slices white bread
6 Tbsp. white glue
1/2 tsp. detergent or 2 tsp. glycerine
Food colouring

Remove the crusts from white bread and knead them with glue plus either detergent or glycerine. Knead mixture until no longer sticky. Separate into portions and tint with food colouring. Shape and brush with equal parts glue and water for a smooth appearance. Let dry overnight to harden. Use acrylic paints, acrylic spray or clear nail polish to seal and preserve.

Baker's Clay

    4 cups flour
    1 cup salt
    1 tsp. powdered alum
    1-1/2 cups water
    Food colouring (optional)

Mix all ingredients in a large bowl. If the dough is too dry, work in another tablespoon of water with your hands. Dough can be coloured by dividing it into several parts and kneading a drop or two of food colouring into each part. Roll or mold as desired.

To Roll: Roll dough 1/8" thick on lightly floured board. Cut with cookie cutters dipped in flour. Make a hole in the top, 1/4" down, for hanging, by using the end of a plastic straw dipped in flour. Shake the dots of clay from the straw and press on as decorations.

To Mold: Shape dough no more than 1/2" thick into figures such as flowers, fruits, animals, etc. Insert a fine wire in each for hanging.

Bake ornaments on ungreased cookie sheet for about 30 minutes in a 250° oven. Turn and bake another 1-1/2 hours until hard and dry. Remove and cool. When done, sand lightly with fine sandpaper until smooth. Paint with plastic-based poster paint, acrylic paint or markers. Paint both sides. Allow paint to dry and seal with clear shellac, acrylic spray or clear nail polish.

This recipe makes about 5 dozen 2-1/2" ornaments.

No-Bake Craft Clay

    1 cup cornstarch
    1-1/4 cups cold water
    2 cups baking soda (1 lb.)
    Food colouring (optional)
    Paints (optional)

Stir in a saucepan over medium heat for about 4 minutes until the mixture thickens to moist mashed potato consistency. For colour, add a few drops of food colouring to the water before it is mixed with starch and soda. Remove from heat, turn out onto a plate and cover with a damp cloth until cool. Knead as you would dough. Shape as desired or store in an airtight container or plastic bag. Objects may be left to dry then painted with tempera paints or acrylics. Dip in shellac, spray with clear acrylic or brush with clear nail polish to seal.

No-Bake Cookie Clay

These ornaments are not edible!

> 2 cups salt
> 2/3 cup water
> 1 cup cornstarch
> 1/2 cup cold water

Mix salt with 2/3 cup water in a medium saucepan. Stir and boil. Add cornstarch and 1/2 cup cold water and stir. If it doesn't get thick, set back on the stove. Use extra cornstarch on table and rolling pin. Roll out dough and cut with cookie cutters. Use straw for making hole at the top for hanging. Dry and decorate with paint, glitter, etc.

GLUE & PASTE

The following glue and paste recipes use different ingredients and are made using different methods. Choose the one that best suits your project of the day. For variety, add food colouring to glue before using. Store all products in an airtight container in the refrigerator.

Glue

> 3/4 cup water
> 2 Tbsp. corn syrup
> 1 tsp. white vinegar
> 1/2 cup cornstarch
> 3/4 cup cold water

Mix water, corn syrup and white vinegar in a small saucepan. Bring to a full, rolling boil. In a small bowl, mix cornstarch with cold water. Add this mixture slowly to the hot mixture, stirring constantly. Let stand overnight before using.

Glass Glue

2 packages unflavoured gelatin
2 Tbsp. cold water
3 Tbsp. skimmed milk

Empty unflavoured gelatin into cold water. Stir and set aside to soften. Heat skimmed milk to a boil and pour over gelatin. Stir thoroughly until dissolved. Apply to objects with a brush while the glue is still warm. This glue is waterproof and can be used for almost anything, but does not store well so is really only good for the day you make it.

Homemade Paste

1/2 cup flour
Cold water

Add some cold water to the 1/2 cup flour until it is as thick as cream. Simmer and stir on stove for 5 minutes. Add a few drops of flavouring and/or food colouring if desired. This makes a wet, messy paste that takes a while to dry. This is a good paste to use when pasting for the love of it.

Papier Mâché Paste

1 cup water
1/4 cup flour
5 cups lightly boiling water

Mix the flour into 1 cup water until the mixture is thin and runny. Stir this mixture into the lightly boiling water. Gently boil and stir for 2 to 3 minutes. Cool before using. (See Chapter 8 for additional information on papier mâché.)

Library Paste

1 cup flour
1 cup sugar
1 tsp. alum
4 cups water
Oil of cloves

Mix all ingredients in a saucepan and cook until clear and thick. Add 30 drops oil of cloves and store covered.

No-Cook Paste

1/2 cup flour
Water
Salt

Mix flour with water until gooey. Add a pinch of salt and stir.

OTHER CRAFT RECIPES

Use the following recipes to make interesting materials for use in various art and craft projects.

Colourful Creative Salt

1/2 cup salt
5-6 drops food colouring

Add food colouring to salt and stir well. Cook in microwave for 1-2 minutes or spread on waxed paper and let air dry. Store in an airtight container. Use as you would glitter.

Pasta Dye

1/2 cup rubbing alcohol
Food colouring

Mix alcohol and food colouring in bowl. Add small amounts of each type of pasta to the liquid and gently mix. The larger the pasta the longer it takes to absorb the colour. Dry on newspapers covered with wax paper.

Egg Dye

1/4 tsp. food colouring
3/4 cup hot water
1 Tbsp. white vinegar

Measure liquids into bowl or cup and mix, using different food colouring for each colour desired. Soak eggs until the desired shade is obtained. (See Easter activities in Chapter 9 for additional information on egg dyes and decorating.)

Ornamental Frosting

This frosting works like an edible glue; use for gingerbread houses or other food projects that you want to be able to eat!

    3 egg whites
    1 tsp. cream of tartar
    1 lb. sifted icing sugar (about 4 cups)

Beat egg whites with cream of tartar until stiff peaks form. Add sifted icing sugar and continue beating until mixture is thick and holds its shape. Cover with a damp cloth when not in use. This can be made several hours or the day before using; store in an airtight container in the refrigerator.

3.

Rainy Day Play

"The years rush past, as every older woman will tell the young mothers who complain that they still have two little ones at home and it seems like forever before they will all be in school. Oh no, they say--time flies--enjoy them while they're young--they grow up so fast ...

The mothers agree that indeed the years do fly. It's the days that don't. The hours, minutes of a single day sometimes just stop. And a mother finds herself standing in the middle of a room wondering. Wondering. Years fly. Of course they do. But a mother can gag on a day."

Jain Sherrard

Life with preschoolers can be a wonderful, rewarding experience. On long, warm, summer days, when adults and children alike can be outside from sunup to sundown, parenting can seem very fun and uncomplicated. But "fun" and "easy" are not words you are likely to hear from anyone who has endured a week of rain with several housebound preschoolers. Most preschoolers have such a great amount of energy but a relatively short attention span. Boredom can cause acutely irritating behaviour in small children, and should be avoided as much as possible. Now is the time for big, messy art projects (see Chapter 8) and marathon baking sessions. Invite friends for lunch frequently, and always be prepared with something fun for the children to do indoors.

KITCHEN FUN

The following activities are best suited to your kitchen, as most require a table or countertop and some require water. Some activities may also be appropriate elsewhere in your house.

Clean Coins (#1)

> Old toothbrush
> Soap
> Water
> Bowl
> Coins
> Dish cloth or paper towel
> Salt and vinegar (optional)

Your child can practice cleaning coins with an old toothbrush and some soap and water. Fill a bowl with a small amount of water and place a few coins in the bowl. Your child will have fun brushing the coins with soap to make them look brand new. Dry with a dish cloth or paper towel.

For super shiny coins, mix a small amount of salt and vinegar in a bowl. Drop the coins in and watch the tarnish fade.

Super Suds (#2)

> Liquid detergent
> Water
> Bowl
> Eggbeater
> Straw (optional)

Put a few drops of liquid detergent into a bowl and fill it halfway with water. Use an eggbeater to whip up some suds in the soapy water, or a big straw to blow some really big bubbles.

Count the Coins (#3)

> Pennies or other coins

Give your child a jar of pennies or other coins and have her count them and place them in stacks of five or ten. Then count the stacks. Talk to her about what money can and cannot buy by giving her examples to choose from: "Can money buy us food?", "...good friends?", "...clothes?", "...a new baby sister?", etc.

Indoor Sandbox (#4)

Cardboard box or plastic baby bath
Puffed wheat or rice cereal
Sandbox toys

Create an indoor sandbox by filling a cardboard box, plastic baby bath or basin with inexpensive puffed wheat or rice cereal. Use buckets and shovels, dumptrucks, or measuring cups, spoons and bowls. Clean up is easy! (Uncooked rice can be inexpensive when bought in bulk, and provides a more interesting material for small trucks or other wheeled toys to drive through.)

Paper Punch (#5)

Hole puncher
Paper scraps

Give your child a hole puncher and scraps of paper in various colours. She will amuse herself for quite some time making confetti that can be saved and used for art and craft activities.

Sharpen a Pencil (#6)

Pencils or crayons
Pencil or crayon sharpener
Small plate or cup

Your preschooler will no doubt have a lot of fun sharpening pencils. Give her a pencil sharpener, pencil, and a small plate or cup to catch the shavings. For younger children, it is probably better to use crayons and a crayon sharpener.

Write a Story (#7)

Paper
Pen, markers or crayons
Photographs or old magazines
Scissors
Glue

Write a story with your child about events in her life, a story in which she is the central character. Begin the story by saying, for example, "Today is a special day for (child's name) because she is going to _____." Write the story down, including her responses, and illustrate it with drawings, photos, or pictures cut from magazines. She can help you choose and glue in the pictures.

Indoor Tent (#8)

Sheet or blanket
Empty table

Place a sheet or blanket over a table to make an indoor tent. Use flashlights for fun and have a special snack inside, or give your child a pillow and blanket and she may camp out all morning.

What's Missing? (#9)

Various household objects or small toys

Test your preschooler's memory skills by placing a few toys or household objects in front her. Allow her to study them, then have her close her eyes while you remove one object. See if she can tell you which object is missing.

Sticker Play (#10)

Stickers from magazine and record clubs

Save all the stickers that come in the mail, the ones advertising records or magazines. Separate them on the perforated lines and let your child stick them onto a plain piece of paper or decorate her artwork.

Paper Clip Jewellery (#11)

Paper clips

Show your child how to link paper clips together to form a necklace or bracelet. Standard metal clips or bright plastic ones, or a combination of the two, can be used.

Nail Board (#12)

Nails
Wood
Hammer
String or elastic bands

Hammer nails into a piece of board and allow your child to create a design by wrapping string or coloured elastic bands around the nails. Hammer the nails in a pattern, or use rows or circles so your child can create her own design.

Magnet Magic (#13)

Refrigerator magnets
Heavy paper

Give your child a couple of refrigerator magnets and a heavy piece of paper. Place the paper between the two magnets and show her how to move the top magnet by pulling the bottom magnet along. On the top side of the paper draw a road or some other pattern that your child can try to follow.

Lid Art (#14)

Plastic lids from 4-litre milk jugs
Glue
Paper plate or piece of cardboard

If you buy your milk or juice in the 4-litre plastic jug, save the small plastic lids. Once you have a collection of different coloured lids, let your child glue them onto a piece of cardboard or a paper plate to create an interesting design. Kids will also have fun sorting lids by colour or lining them up end to end.

Kitchen Chorus (#15)

Pots and pans with lids
Wooden spoon
Wire whisk
Rubber spatula
Other unbreakable kitchen objects

Give your child a variety of safe, unbreakable kitchen objects so she can make her own symphony; wooden spoons, wire whisks, rubber spatulas, pots and pans with lids, etc. This is a really noisy activity, but sure to keep her busy when you're working to get supper on the table.

I Love You Because ... (#16)

Paper and pen
Crayons or markers

Ask your child "Why do you love Daddy?". Write down her responses on a sheet of plain or construction paper and have your child decorate it with crayons or markers. Place it as a surprise in Dad's lunch the next day. You can do this for grandparents or other friends and relatives. Some of the answers you get may be priceless!

Setting the Table (#17)

    Plates
    Silverware
    Napkins
    Glasses

When you aren't using your best china, your child can help you set the table. Have her count the number of people who will be eating, then count out the same number of knives, forks, spoons, plates, napkins, etc. Show her how to place everything on the table properly.

Musical Glasses (#18)

    Drinking glasses
    Water
    Spoon

Fill drinking glasses with different amounts of water and have your child lightly tap the glasses with a spoon. Notice the different sounds each glass makes. Try to play simple tunes, or make up your own melody as you go.

Memory (#19)

    Index cards
    Pen or marker

Sharpen your preschooler's memory skills by making up your own memory game. Create two identical sets of index cards; some suggestions are letters of the alphabet, colours, shapes, numbers, etc. Start out with only a few, as this can be tough. Place all the cards, face down, on the table. Have your child turn over one card, then try to find the corresponding matching card. You can determine the number of tries allowed, and can make a game out of this between two or more children. At first she may only be guessing, but it won't take long for your child to get the idea.

Little Carpenter (#20)

    Golf tees
    Plastic foam
    Toy hammer

Give your child some golf tees, a toy hammer and a piece of plastic foam. She can hammer the golf tees into the foam in a design, or just hammer for the sake of hammering.

Who Loves You? (#21)

Paper and pen

Ask your child "Who loves you?" and write down her response when she answers. Ask "Who else loves you?" and write down each name, then read her the list when she is finished. Stick it on the refrigerator or on her bedroom wall to remind her how much she is loved.

Fun with Water (#22)

Spoons
Egg beaters
Plastic bowls and dishes

Fill a sink with warm soapy water and let your child play with spoons, a whisk, an egg beater, and plastic bowls and dishes while you work.

Put Away the Silverware (#23)

Silverware
Utensil holder

Your child can help you put away the silverware as you remove it from the dishwasher or drainer. Place your utensil holder on the table with the clean utensils next to it. Your child can then sort, count and put them away.

Washing Windows (#24)

Spray bottle
Water
Vinegar
Cleaning cloth

Fill a spray bottle with water and 1/4 cup white vinegar. Give your child the bottle and cleaning cloth and let her help you wash the windows, bathroom counters, or kitchen appliances. She will love to be your helper and work along side you while you do some cleaning of your own.

Listening Game (#25)

Have your child close her eyes and guess the sounds you make. Use household objects such as keys, coins, silverware, or a whistle. Tap on a pot with a spoon, snap your fingers or click your tongue.

Sewing Practice (#26)

Heavy cardboard
Scissors
Hole punch
Shoelace or yarn
Tape (if using yarn)

Cut a shape out of heavy cardboard and punch holes around the edges and at intervals throughout the card. Tie a knot in one end of an old shoelace, or knot one end of a piece of yarn and wrap heavy tape around the other end. Let your child sew by weaving the shoelace through the punched holes. This fun activity is great for hand-eye coordination.

Wash the Floor (#27)

Bucket of water
Sponge

Give your child a small bucket of water and a sponge and let her help you when you are washing the floor. She will have fun getting water everywhere, and it's easy to clean up!

Surprise Package (#28)

Common household object
Shoe box or other small box
Wrapping paper

Place a common household object inside a shoe box and cover the box with wrapping paper. Give your child three clues that describe the object in the box. Have her guess what it is before opening the package.

Hand Puppets (#29)

Washable markers

Using washable markers, draw a face on the palm of your child's hand, or draw small faces on the pads of each finger so that the puppets can "talk" to each other. Draw puppets on your own fingers and get some conversations going between your puppets and your child's.

IN THE BATHROOM

Kids love to play with water, and will usually jump at the chance for a bath if it includes some special play time. Here are a few suggestions to make bathtime more fun, as well as other activities suitable for the bathroom.

Soap Afloat (#30)

    Bar soap
    Washcloth
    Thread
    Needle
    Buttons (2)

Wrap a washcloth around a bar of soap and sew the open ends together. Sew button eyes on top and let your child lather up in the bath.

Indoor Water Play (#31)

    Eyedropper
    Small containers of water
    Food colouring

Give your child an eyedropper and several small containers of water coloured with a few drops of food colouring. Let her mix colours or drop water into other empty containers.

Bath Paints (#32)

    Shaving cream
    Food colouring
    Muffin tin
    Spoon
    Paint brushes or sponge

This is a real favourite with our children! Squirt shaving cream into the individual sections of a muffin tin. Add a few drops of food colouring to each section and mix with a spoon. The kids will love painting the walls, the tub and themselves with their hands, a sponge, or paint brushes. Older children will enjoy mixing the individual colours to create new ones. Clean up is easy after the fun is over!

Fun with Weights (#33)

Bathroom scale
Various household objects

Using a bathroom scale, weigh your child and help her to weigh different household objects: a stack of books, bag of flour, dolls, etc. Try to find something that weighs the same as your child.

BEDROOM PLAY

These activities are intended for the bedroom, but can be easily adapted for other rooms in your house.

Pillow Throw (#34)

Lots of throw pillows

Have one person sit on a bed or couch with the throw pillows. Have the other person run across the room from one point to another, while the person on the bed tries to hit the moving target with the pillows.

Doll Closet (#35)

Tension rod
Baby clothes hangers

Make a closet for all those little doll clothes by inserting a tension rod across the lower shelf of a bookcase. Doll clothes can be hung on baby clothes hangers and then onto the rod. (Try to save some of your newborn-size clothes, bibs and blankets; they are the perfect size for many dolls.)

Sorting Socks (#36)

Socks
Laundry basket

Take all the socks out of your child's sock drawer. Have her identify each colour as she puts them back in. For some real fun, give your child a laundry basket and have her collect all the socks from every sock drawer in the house. She can amuse herself for a long time by sorting them by colour, size, or who they belong to.

Shape Shake (#37)

Cardboard
Scissors
String

Cut out a cardboard shape and pierce a small hole in the center. Tie one end of a string to the doorknob of your child's room and thread the opposite end of the string through the shape's hole. Have your child stand across the room holding the free end of the string. See how long it takes her to shake the shape from one end to the other.

Sort the Laundry (#38)

Laundry

This is a great activity that will give your child some household responsibility and teach a very practical skill at the same time. Show your child how to sort the laundry before you wash it. Even a very young child can separate whites, colours, and darks, and it will save you time as well! You can also have your child remove the clothes from the dryer, and sort and carry them to the appropriate rooms when folded. Folding may be a little tricky depending on your standards, but you can let her tackle the easy things: towels, dish cloths, baby blankets, etc.

Sock Toss (#39)

Soft ball or rolled up socks
Empty laundry basket

Using rolled up socks or a small soft ball, place an empty laundry basket on the floor and have your child toss the ball or socks into the basket from several feet away. Place the basket on top of a dresser for a game of indoor basketball.

IN THE FAMILY ROOM

Most of these activities require some floor space and are suitable for your family room, playroom, living room or basement.

Carpet Raceway (#40)

Books or scraps of wood
Matchbox cars or other toys with wheels

Make a raceway or train track on a carpet by laying down books of equal thickness, or use pieces of plywood or two-by-four. This will transform the carpet into a smooth surface for racing toys with wheels.

Hotter/Colder (#41)

Small toys or edible treats

Hide several household objects, small toys or edible treats around the house and encourage your child to find them. Tell her she is "hotter" when she is closer to the hidden item, "colder" as she moves away from it.

Living Room Picnic (#42)

Tablecloth
Picnic dishes
Picnic food
Summer clothing

The coldest, rainiest or stormiest of days can be brightened by having an indoor picnic. Spread a tablecloth on the floor of your living room and use outdoor dishes or paper plates. Picnic-type dress (shorts or a bathing suit) is essential, and don't forget your sunglasses.

Indoor Camping (#43)

Sleeping bags
Marshmallows

Don't let the weather stop you--to a preschooler, indoor camping can be just as fun, and surely more adventurous! Lay out the sleeping bags in front of the fireplace, if you have one. Eat marshmallows and sing campfire songs. Strum on a guitar if you can, and turn the night into a precious memory for you and your child.

Night at the Movies (#44)

Family video or favourite movie
Special snack

Whether your child watches a little television or a lot, you can still make an occasion out of watching a special program or movie together. Snuggle under a blanket or lie on the floor. Dim the lights and have a special snack together.

Hide and Seek (#45)

Kitchen timer

Wind up your kitchen timer and hide it somewhere in the house. Have your child search for it by listening for its ticking sound.

Fishing (#46)

Construction paper
Scissors
Pen, crayon or marker
Small box or container

Cut fish shapes out of different colours of construction paper. On each fish write a different instruction: "find something red", "count to ten", "touch your toes", etc. Place the fish in a pot and let your child pick out one fish at a time. Read the instruction and have her perform it.

Tell Me a Story (#47)

Various household objects
Pillowcase or brown paper bag

Put five or six various household objects into a brown paper bag or pillow case: keys, purse, stuffed animal, book, etc. Remove each item from the bag one at a time, and create a story by adding one sentence for each item as it is removed: "Once upon a time there was a *little white kitten* named Angel. Angel just loved to read *books*, especially books about *cookies*."

Red Light/Green Light (#48)

Stand 20 or 25 feet away from your child. When you say "green light", she walks, runs, hops, skips or crawls toward you. She must stop when you say "red light".

Balancing Board (#49)

Board measuring about 8" wide by 6' long
Magazines or other books

Place a board about 8" wide and 6' long across two piles of magazines. Your child will have fun practicing keeping her balance by walking across the board. As your child grows more steady, you can place one end on a chair and she can walk up it, or across two chairs as she grows even more bold.

Chair Maze (#50)

Chairs

This activity will work well outdoors or in. Place chairs in a maze around the room. Let your child crawl through them or walk over them, or use them as a train for her stuffed animals.

Make a Tape (#51)

Tape recorder
Blank cassette tape

If you have access to a tape recorder, help your child make a tape for Dad to play on his way to work. Sing favourite songs, say nursery rhymes, tell him a story, talk about what you do when he's at work, tell him you love him and why you're thankful for him. This makes a great Father's Day gift, or you can use this idea for a grandparent or other special person who may live near or far away.

Animal Charades (#52)

Stuffed animals
Pillowcase

Using a variety of different stuffed animals, place several in a pillowcase and close your eyes while your child takes one out and looks at it. Have her put it back in the case, then act out the animal while you try to guess what it is.

Follow the Leader (#53)

Have your child follow you through the house, imitating the sounds and movements you make. You can dance around, pretend to be a bunny or a horse, a train or a car, etc. Take turns and let your child lead you.

Pretend Islands (#54)

Pillows

Place pillows on the carpet for pretend islands, and pretend the carpet is the ocean. Have your child jump from island to island without falling in the water.

Bean Bag Toss (#55)

Scraps of material
Needle and thread
Dried beans

Make a homemade bean bag by sewing together two 4" squares of material. Leave a small space on the fourth side and fill the bag with dried beans, then sew up the space. Use the beanbag to play catch, or have your child toss the bag into an empty laundry basket from a few feet away.

Shoe Trail (#56)

Empty laundry basket
Shoes

Give your child a laundry basket and have her fill it with shoes. Make a trail of shoes around the house, lining them up heel to toe. Follow the trail, counting as you go. Keep a list, and have your child count how many shoes each person has, or how many shoes of each colour there are, or how many shoes there are in total. Help your child put them away when done.

Go Fish (#57)

Stick for fishing pole
String
Magnet
Scissors
Construction paper
Glue or tape
Metal paper clips

Cut fish shapes out of construction paper. Glue or tape metal paper clips to the back of each fish. Make a fishing pole out of a long stick and a length of string. Tie a magnet on the end of the string and go fishing. This works well if you place the "fish" on the floor and let your child fish over the back of the couch.

Indoor Treasure Hunt (#58)

Small toys or snacks
Treasure map (optional)

This is a great way to liven up a rainy day. Have an indoor treasure hunt by hiding several small toys, books or special snacks around the house. Give your child clues or draw a map that leads to the treasure.

Play with Boxes (#59)

Cardboard boxes in various sizes

Your child can put supermarket boxes of all sizes to good use. She can have a train for herself or her animals, build a fort, make a dollhouse, or ride in a car. You can be sure she will think of something new every time.

Simon Says (#60)

This is a fun game to play with your child. Have your child follow your actions only when you say "Simon says": "Simon says touch your toes", "Simon says stretch your arms", "Simon says jump up and down". Your child should remain motionless when you give a command that is not preceded by "Simon says": "Turn around". This is a lot of fun when done very quickly, and is a good game for a group. You can have each child sit down if they move when they're not supposed to, and award a small prize to the last child left standing. Take turns being Simon.

Whose Ear Is This? (#61)

Blindfold

For this activity you will need at least three people. Take turns blindfolding each other and try to guess who each person is just by touching one feature- the nose, finger, ear, hair, or whatever.

4.

Kids in the Kitchen

"You cannot teach a child to take care of himself unless you let him try to take care of himself. He will make mistakes; and out of these mistakes will come his wisdom."

Francis Bacon

Work and play are inseparable for kids; your work is very often your child's play. Undoubtedly you spend a lot of your work time in the kitchen, and your child will naturally want to be with you. The kitchen is home to many interesting things that may prove irresistable for your child. Make sure any dangerous objects are well out of reach, and consider providing your child with his very own *Baker's Box* (see Chapter 1). Try to provide a different kitchen activity as often as possible (see also the *Kitchen Fun* section in Chapter 3). Getting dinner on the table at the "arsenic hour" will be less of an ordeal if you make special plans to keep your child busy.

FUN WITH FOOD

Anyone who has ever watched a small child eat will know that as much as food is meant to be eaten, to a child it is also something to be played with. Children, even as young as two, will enjoy making their own peanut butter sandwiches, and most will agree that finger jello is one of the best foods ever invented. Accept that things may get a little messy, and let your child enjoy his food experience.

Fruit Kebabs (#62)

Small wooden skewers, popsicle sticks, coffee stirrers or swizzle sticks
Various types of fruit

Cut up pieces of fruit and have your child create fruit kebabs by putting pieces on small wooden skewers, wooden popsicle sticks, plastic coffee stirrers or swizzle sticks. Talk about the different types of fruit, their colours, smells and tastes. Serve for dessert or a tasty snack.

Taste Testing (#63)

Blindfold
Various food items

Blindfold your child and have him identify by taste and smell some of his favourite foods (ice cream, pickles, yogurt, cereal, cookies, etc.). Have him describe the different tastes and textures and ask him to group them as sweet, salty, bitter, sour, spicy or tangy.

Melon Bowl (#64)

Watermelon
Other melons (honeydew, cantelope, etc.)
Knife
Melon ball scoop

Make a watermelon bowl by cutting the watermelon in half. Have your child scoop out the melon with a melon ball scoop. Cut open several other melons and have him continue to make more melon balls. Fill the watermelon bowl with the melon balls and serve as a summer dessert or tasty afternoon snack.

Happy Face Sandwich (#65)

Bread
Peanut butter
Raisins or chocolate chips
Knife

Spread peanut butter on one side of a piece of bread. Have your child make eyes, a nose and a big, happy smile with raisins or chocolate chips.

Flour Drawing (#66)

Cookie sheet
Flour

Lightly sprinkle the surface of a cookie sheet with flour. Show your child how to draw with his finger. Or draw a letter, number or shape with your own finger and have him draw the same next to yours.

Pudding Paints (#67)

Packaged pudding mix

Prepare packaged pudding mix ahead of time, and when cooled allow your child to fingerpaint on a plastic or paper plate, tabletop, or other smooth surface. This may not be suitable before a meal, but there probably won't be much left to clean up!

Mini-Popsicles (#68)

Empty ice cube tray
Juice
Fruit (grapes, raisins, cherries)
Toothpicks

Fill an empty ice cube tray with juice and put one or two pieces of fruit (grapes, raisins and cherries work well) and one toothpick inside each compartment. Freeze and enjoy.

Homemade Peanut Butter (#69)

Peanuts in the shell
Food processor
Small container or baby food jar

Shelling enough peanuts to make a little peanut butter is sure to keep your child busy. Place the shelled peanuts in your food processor and process until smooth. Store in a covered container. To give as a gift, place peanut butter in a small baby food jar with lid. Tie a circle of fabric around the neck of the jar with a ribbon.

Pasta Play (#70)

Dried pasta
Measuring cups
Empty bowls
Mixing spoons

Give your child containers filled with different sizes and shapes of dried pasta, i.e. macaroni, rotini, shells, etc. Add a few empty bowls, measuring cups and a mixing spoon or two and your child can cook up some wonderful delights. For a little variation, try using cereal, dried beans, rice or water in place of pasta.

Banana Balls (#71)

Ripe bananas
Bowl
Fork
Finely chopped nuts
Cinnamon
Cookie sheet

Have your child mash up a ripe banana in a bowl with a fork. Add finely chopped nuts and a dash of cinnamon, and mix. Form the mixture into balls by rolling a small amount and placing it on a cookie sheet. When all the balls are complete, cover the cookie sheet and refrigerate until it is time for eating. These are great for a quick snack or for floating in cereal and milk for breakfast.

Leftovers (#72)

Measuring cups
Empty bowls
Mixing spoons

This is a great activity for the day before "Garbage Day" when you rid your refrigerator of its most questionable contents. Instead of just throwing the food away, place it in the kitchen sink. Give your child a chair to stand on and some measuring cups, spoons and empty bowls. Let him mix, measure, add water or do whatever he wants with "his food". You can throw it away when he's had enough.

Apple Shapes (#73)

Apples
Cookie cutters
Knife

Peel apples and cut into slices. Give your child small cookie cutters and let him cut shapes out of the slices.

Chase the Pepper (#74)

Pie plate or small sink
Pepper
Bar of soap
Sugar

Your child will love to show off this neat trick. Fill a pie plate or small sink with water. Shake pepper on the water and dip a piece of wet soap into it. The pepper will run away from the soap. Now shake some sugar into the clear area and the pepper will run back.

COOKING WITH KIDS

The kitchen is a tantalizing place for children, full of wonderful things to smell, touch and taste. With a little bit of effort and a lot of patience on your part, it can also become a wonderful classroom for your child. Talk to him about the magic of the kitchen, how yeast or baking powder makes things rise, how the batter baked in the oven turns into a cake, how cornstarch thickens a sauce. He will want to help you measure and mix, wash vegetables, cut out cookies, and sift dry ingredients. Include him in your work and take the time to teach him as you go. Make or buy your child his own recipe box and copy out his favourite recipes, using simple words, pictures and symbols. Include some simple "no-cook" recipes that he can make with little supervision.

Animal Pancakes (#75)

1-1/4 cups all-purpose flour
2 Tbsp. sugar
2 tsp. baking powder

3/4 tsp. salt
3 Tbsp. salad oil
1-1/3 cups milk
1 egg, slightly beaten

In large bowl, with fork, mix first four ingredients; add salad oil, milk and egg and stir just until flour is moistened. Preheat electric griddle or skillet and brush lightly with salad oil. Drop the batter into the pan and use a spoon to make animal shapes. A bunny needs only a round shape for the head and two long shapes for ears (and maybe chocolate chips or blueberries for eyes). Try a mouse with an oval body, smaller drops for the head, ears and feet, and a long thin tail. A turtle can be one big spoonful of batter surrounded by six smaller drops. Try a cat, bird, giraffe, elephant ... use your imagination!

Snow-Topped Cupcakes (#76)

1 egg
1 cup milk
1 tsp. vanilla
1-1/4 cup white sugar
1/2 cup margarine, melted
1-3/4 cup flour
2-1/2 tsp. baking powder
1/2 tsp. salt
White frosting
Shredded coconut

Blend the egg, milk, vanilla, sugar and margarine on medium speed with electric mixer. Add flour, baking powder and salt and mix on the top speed of mixer for 2 minutes. Pour into paper-lined muffin tins. Bake at 350○ for 20 minutes. Let your child frost them with white icing and dip them in coconut for the snow on top. Serve them for dinner or at a teddy-bear tea.

Alphabet Cookies (#77)

This special vanilla dough handles like modelling clay, but also makes delicious cookies. Use this activity to strengthen your child's alphabet skills. The finished product makes a good placecard for birthday parties.

4-1/2 cups unsifted all-purpose flour
1-1/2 cups butter
3 hard-cooked egg yolks
3/4 cup sugar
3 raw egg yolks
1-1/2 tsp. vanilla

Measure flour into mixing bowl. Add butter which has been cut into small pieces. Mix with your fingers until the flour and butter form fine crumbs. Mash cooked egg yolks with sugar and stir into the flour mixture. Blend raw egg yolks with vanilla and stir into the flour mixture with a fork. Press the mixture with your hands into a firm ball. Keep the ball covered. Work with the dough at room temperature, but refrigerate it if you make it ahead.

Roll out the dough. Cut 3" or 4" strips that you can roll with your palm to make ropes. Shape the ropes into letters. Flatten them slightly so they are about 1/4" thick. If you like, decorate the letters with colored sugar or chocolate. Bake at 300° for 25-30 minutes.

Paintbox Cookies (#78)

These sturdy cookies, baked and glazed ahead, can be painted with food colouring for a rainy day or party project.

2 cups softened butter or margarine
2 cups granulated sugar
2 tsp. vanilla
5 cups flour
5-9 tsp. warm water
1-1/2 lb. icing sugar
Food colouring

Beat butter, granulated sugar and vanilla together. Add flour and mix until thoroughly blended. Roll dough out on ungreased baking sheet to 1/4-3/8" thickness. Cut in shapes with a knife or floured cookie cutters. Bake at 300° for 25-30 minutes until dough is a pale golden colour. Let cookies cool on pan about 7 minues, then transfer to foil-covered surface.

To make icing, add warm water to icing sugar until icing is smooth and thick. Spread cookies with icing to make smooth surface. Don't cover or disturb until icing is dry to touch (8 to 24 hours).

Paint with food colouring when dry. Use a brush and small cups of food colouring undiluted for bright colours or slightly diluted for lighter ones. Food colouring will flow, so allow each colour to dry briefly before adding the next.

May store at room temperature for up to 4 days or freeze for longer storage. Thaw before painting.

Cookie Cut-Outs (#79)

This is the tastiest rolled cookie recipe I've found

2-1/2 cups flour
1 tsp. cinnamon
1/2 tsp ginger, optional
1/2 tsp. baking powder
1/4 tsp. soda
1/4 tsp. salt
3/4 cup butter
1/2 cup liquid honey
1/3 cup granulated sugar
1 egg

Stir together flour, cinnamon, ginger, baking powder, baking soda and salt. Set aside. Cream together butter, honey and sugar until smooth. Beat in egg. Stir in flour mixture, mixing well. Cover and refrigerate dough for 1-1/2 hours or until firm enough to roll and cut.

Roll out on well floured surface, about one-third of the dough at a time. Cut into desired shapes using floured cutters. Place on lightly greased cookie sheets. Bake for 8 to 10 minutes at 350° until lightly browned and firm to touch. Makes 3 to 4 dozen cookies.

You can decorate these with coloured sugar or sprinkles before baking, or when cool ice with butter icing and then decorate.

Best Chocolate Chip Cookies in the World (#80)

This makes a truly great chocolate chip cookie. Make sure the batter is cold before baking, and don't overbake them because they do harden as they cool.

1/2 cup margarine, room temperature
1/2 cup unsalted butter, room temperature
1 cup packed dark brown sugar
1 cup granulated sugar
2 eggs, lightly beaten
2 Tbsp. milk
2 tsp. vanilla extract
2 cups sifted all-purpose flour
1 tsp. baking powder
1 tsp. baking soda
1 tsp. salt
2 cups quick-cooking oats
1 cup (or more) chocolate chips
1 cup coarsely chopped walnuts

Cream the margarine, butter and both sugars in a large mixer bowl until light and fluffy. Add the eggs, milk, and vanilla and beat until blended. Sift the flour, baking powder, baking soda, and salt together and add to the butter mixture. Stir just until blended. Stir in the oats. Fold in the chocolate and walnuts. Refrigerate the dough covered for at least one hour.

Preheat oven to 350°. Grease cookie sheets. Shape the dough into balls, using a rounded teaspoon for small cookies or a scant tablespoon for large. Flatten slightly into rounded disks. Place 2 inches apart on the prepared baking sheets. Bake until the edges are slightly browned but the cookies are still white, 8 to 10 minutes. Remove from the oven and let cool on the sheets for 5 minutes. Remove to wire racks to cool completely.

Aggression Cookies (#81)

This is truly one recipe your child can make all by himself.

  3 cups oatmeal
  1-1/2 cups brown sugar
  1-1/2 cups flour
  1-1/2 cups butter or margarine
  1-1/2 tsp. baking powder

Dump all the ingredients into a large bowl and let your child really go at it! Pound it, punch it, knead it ... the longer and harder it is mixed, the better it will taste! When ready to bake, roll dough into small balls and bake on ungreased cookie sheet at 350° for 10-12 minutes.

Peanut Butter Oat Squares (#82)

  1/2 cup butter, softened
  1 cup lightly packed brown sugar
  1/2 cup corn syrup
  1 tsp. salt
  2 tsp. vanilla
  4 cups oats
  1/2 cup peanut butter
  1/2 cup chocolate chips
  1-1/2 tsp. butter

Cream butter and brown sugar. Add corn syrup, salt, vanilla and oats. Mix well. Spread mixture evenly in greased 9"x13" pan. Bake at 350° for 15 minutes. Cool slightly. Spread peanut butter evenly over top. Melt chocolate chips and butter together until smooth. Drizzle over peanut butter. Cool to set chocolate, then cut into squares.

Fantastic Fudge Brownies (#83)

Everyone loves a brownie! This is a great rainy day project and something a friend or neighbour will really appreciate.

1 cup butter
2 cups sugar
4 heaping Tbsp. cocoa
4 eggs, beaten
1 cup flour
1 cup walnuts, chopped
1 tsp. vanilla
Icing:
2 cups icing sugar
2 Tbsp. butter
2 Tbsp. cocoa
2 Tbsp. boiling water
2 tsp. vanilla

Cream sugar, cocoa and butter. Add beaten eggs and vanilla. Add flour and fold in walnuts. Bake in greased 9"x13" pan at 350° for 40 to 45 minutes. Top will appear to be underdone (falls in middle) but don't overcook. Should be moist and chewy. Add icing *immediately* after removing from oven so it will melt into a shiny glaze.

Icing: Mix ingredients together with electric beater while brownies are cooking.

Chocolate Pizza Pie (#84)

1-3/4 cup semi-sweet chocolate chips (divided)
1/2 cup golden flavour shortening
1/2 cup all-purpose flour
1/2 cup granulated sugar
2 eggs
1 tsp. baking powder
2 Tbsp. golden flavour shortening
2 Tbsp. water
Assorted candy for decoration

Melt 1 cup chocolate chips and 1/2 cup shortening over hot water; cool. Stir in flour, sugar, eggs and baking powder with fork; mix well. Spread evenly onto well greased 12-inch pizza pan. Bake in 375° oven 15 minutes. Cool. Combine 3/4 cup chocolate chips, 2 Tbsp. shortening, and 2 Tbsp. water in small bowl. Melt over hot water; stir to combine. Spread glaze evenly over cooled chocolate pizza. Decorate as desired with candies.

Peanut Butter Cups (#85)

This is a very easy and tasty recipe that kids can make themselves with a little help.

    2 cups carob chips
    2 cups peanut butter
    3 cups Rice Krispies

Roll the rice cereal between wax paper until it is a powdery texture. Melt the carob chips over a double boiler, then add the peanut butter and cereal powder. Mix well together. Spread the mixture into pie plates and cool in the fridge to harden.

Popcorn Ball Creatures (#86)

    3/4 cup sugar
    1 tsp. white vinegar
    3/4 cup brown sugar
    1/2 cup light corn syrup
    1/2 cup water
    1/4 tsp. salt
    3/4 cup butter
    8 cups popped popcorn

Stir all ingredients except popcorn and butter in a pan over medium heat until the mixture reaches 260° on a candy thermometer (hard ball stage). Reduce temperature to low; add butter. Put popcorn in a large bowl. Pour the mixture over it until it is coated. Cool slightly. Butter your child's hands and let him mold it into animal shapes. Place shapes on wax paper until ready to eat.

Crunch and Munch (#87)

This is a wonderful snack to munch on as you watch your favourite movie, television show or home video together.

    1/2 cup butter or margarine, melted
    1/2 cup honey
    1 cup chopped nuts or peanuts
    12 cups popped popcorn

Combine melted butter or margarine and honey in a small saucepan; heat until well blended. Add chopped nuts. Pour over popcorn and mix well. Spread popcorn mixture in a thin layer on a cookie sheet and bake in 350° oven for 12 minutes until crisp. Stir often to avoid burning.

Rice Krispie Pops (#88)

A new way to serve an old favourite!

5 cups Rice Krispies
1/4 cup margarine or butter
4 cups mini-marshmallows
Wooden popsicle sticks

Melt margarine in a 3-quart saucepan, then add 4 cups marshmallows and cook over low heat, stirring constantly, until syrupy. Remove from heat, add cereal and stir until well coated. Shape an oval around a wooden popsicle stick.

To make Rice Krispie Tarts: prepare recipe as above. Add cereal and stir until well coated. Press into a buttered muffin tin to form a tart shell; fill with fresh fruit or ice cream.

Popsicles (#89)

1 pkg. Kool-Aid
1 pkg. Jello
1-1/4 cups sugar
3/4 cup hot water
3/4 cup cold water

Mix dry ingredients thoroughly. Measure 6 Tbsp. dry ingredients into a mixing bowl; add hot water and cold water. Pour into popsicle moulds and freeze. Store remaining dry ingredients in an airtight container.

Lollipops (#90)

1/4 cup butter
3/4 cup sugar
1/2 cup light corn syrup
Food colouring

Evenly space 16 popsicle sticks on a buttered cookie sheet. In a saucepan, heat butter, sugar and corn syrup over medium high heat; stir until it boils. Reduce heat to medium. Cook until mixture reaches 270° on a candy thermometer, stirring often. Add food colouring. Drop mixture by tablespoons onto the end of each stick. When the lollipops are cool, take them off the sheet and wrap them in plastic wrap.

Finger Jello (#91)

The following *Finger Jello* recipes make use of different ingredients but give basically the same result. Use the recipe that best suits the ingredients you have on hand or prefer to use.

Gelatine/Jello Recipe

This recipe uses a combination of unflavoured gelatine and commercial jelly powder.

> 2 envelopes unflavoured gelatine
> 6 oz. package Jello
> 2-1/2 cups water

Dissolve unflavoured gelatine in one cup cold water. Set aside. In a saucepan, bring 1 cup of water to a boil and add Jello. Bring to a boil and remove from heat. Add gelatine mixture. Stir and add 1/2 cup cold water. Pour into lightly greased pan and set in refrigerator until solid (2 hours). Use cookie cutters or a sharp knife to cut into shapes.

Gelatine/Juice Recipe

Avoid using commercial jelly powder by trying this recipe instead.

> 3 envelopes unflavoured gelatine
> 1 - 12 oz. can frozen juice concentrate
> 12 oz. water

Soften gelatine in the thawed juice and bring water to a boil. Add the juice/gelatine mixture to the boiling water and stir until gelatine is dissolved. Add sugar for extra sweetening, if desired. Pour into lightly greased pan and set in refrigerator until solid (2 hours). Use cookie cutters or a sharp knife to cut into shapes.

Jello Only Recipe

This recipe does not require unflavoured gelatine.

> 2 - 6 oz. packages Jello
> 2-1/2 cups water

Dissolve Jello in 2-1/2 cups boiling water. Pour into lightly greased pan and set in refrigerator until solid (about 3 hours). Use cookie cutters or a knife to cut into shapes.

5.

Out and About

"Any adult who spends even fifteen minutes with a child outdoors finds himself drawn back to his own childhood, like Alice falling down the rabbit hole."

Sharon MacLatchie

Children of all ages have such an endless amount of energy. Outdoor play every day, in almost any weather, is essential. Most children are as happy all bundled up for the snow as they are in shorts in the summertime. Rain provides countless opportunities for play, whether walking beneath an umbrella or stomping in the puddles, and a brisk walk is appropriate almost anytime. Playing outdoors in all types of weather is great fun for kids. You should encourage your child's outdoor play every day, and join her whenever you can.

OUTDOOR ADVENTURES

The following suggestions will provide your preschooler with some fun and interesting things to do outdoors. Most activities require a minimum of materials, and you will find that by making slight adaptations, most are suitable for any season and any weather.

Sidewalk Drawing (#92)

Chalk

Using white or coloured chalk, have your child draw on the sidewalk. There is special sidewalk chalk available, but regular chalk will do ... just be sure to have lots as it wears down pretty quickly.

Paint the House (#93)

Paintbrush
Bucket of water
Painter's cap

Give your child a clean paintbrush, a bucket full of water and a painter's cap and let him paint the outside of the house, the car, or the sidewalks.

Sandpaper Play (#94)

Sandpaper
Wood scraps
Glue (optional)
Paint or markers (optional)

Give your child a piece of sandpaper and some small wood scraps. Show him how to sand the wood, and talk about the difference in how rough and well-sanded wood feels. You may want your child to wear gloves for this activity. Sanded scraps of wood can be glued together and painted or decorated with markers to create a wood sculpture.

Bubble Solution (#95)

2 cups warm water
1 cup liquid dishwashing soap
1/4 cup glycerine
1 tsp. sugar
Funnel, straws, six-pack plastic beverage holders,
    or other unbreakable household objects

Mix together water, dishwashing soap, glycerine and sugar. Use different unbreakable objects found around the house to blow spectacular bubbles; funnels, straws, six-pack beverage holders. Dip them in the bubble solution and blow through them, or wave them through the air like a wand. Store solution in a plastic container with a tight-fitting lid.

Bubble Pipe (#96)

Paper cup
Straw
Dish detergent
Water
Food colouring

Help your child make this simple bubble pipe. Poke a pencil hole 1" from the bottom of a paper cup and stick a drinking straw through it, halfway into the cup. Pour dish detergent into the cup until the straw is covered. Add a little water and a few drops of food colouring. Blow gently until beautiful coloured bubbles froth over the rim of the cup and fill the air.

Backyard Camping (#97)

Tent
Sleeping bags
Pillows
Flashlight
Snack

You don't have to go far to give your preschooler the outdoor experience. On a fine summer night, set up your tent in the backyard. Go for a walk in the dark. Where fires aren't allowed, have a flashlight campfire, a snack and a sing-along before you pile into your sleeping bags for the night.

Obstacle Course (#98)

Miscellaneous outdoor objects

Use a variety of outdoor objects to create an obstacle course your child can run around. Have him run around one way, then in reverse. You can time him as he runs, or he can race with siblings and friends.

Bird Watching (#99)

Notebook
Pen or pencil
Bird book (optional)

Go for a walk with your child and see how many different types of birds you can spot. Take a notebook and write down the ones you see. If you can't identify a bird, write down its description and look it up at the library.

Backyard Picnic (#100)

Blanket
Picnic food
Outdoor toys

You don't have to trek to the park to have a picnic. Try setting up a picnic in your own backyard. Bring out the balls and other outdoor toys to complete the fun. In warmer weather, turn on the sprinkler for some water play.

Hopscotch (#101)

Hopscotch grid
Marker

Hopscotch is a good game for counting, coordination, balance, and improving physical agility (and it's a lot of fun, too). Look for a hopscotch grid at the local schoolyard or draw one on the sidewalk with chalk. Give your child a marker (a small chain works well), and show him how to throw it onto each consecutively numbered square. Hop on one foot to the end of the grid and back again, but be careful not to hop in the square where the marker lays.

Walk in the Dark (#102)

Flashlight
Wagon or stroller (optional)

For children, there is something almost magical about walking in the dark. Bring flashlights with you, and a stroller or wagon for younger children.

Watch the Sunset (#103)

Blanket
Snack

On a warm summer night, take a blanket and a special snack and go to a place where you can watch the sunset.

Mud Painting (#104)

Paintbrush
Mud

Give your child a paintbrush and have him dip it in some mud and draw pictures or write words on the sidewalk. He will have fun hosing it off later, or you can leave it for the next rainfall.

Ice Blocks (#105)

Cardboard milk cartons
Water
Tempera paint

Mix tempera paint with water and freeze in cardboard milk cartons to make large, coloured ice blocks. You can freeze them outside if it's cold enough, or use your freezer if you have the room. (You can make smaller blocks by freezing coloured water in clean plastic food containers or ice cube trays.) Stick the blocks together with water and show your child how to build a wall. It will last a long time if placed out of direct sunlight and temperatures remain below freezing.

Wash the Dishes (#106)

Baby bathtub or large basin
Water
Miscellaneous non-breakable household items
Child's toys and play dishes
Soap (optional)

On a warm day set a tub of water on the deck or in the backyard and fill it with plastic cups, funnels, straws, sponges, sieves, etc. For variety, add a little soap and let your child wash his toys or dishes.

Quiet Time (#107)

Blanket
Books
Pillows (optional)

After lunch on a hot summer day, spread out your blanket in a shady spot under a nearby tree. Take your child's favourite books, something cool to drink, and maybe a pillow for a leisurely nap.

Slip and Slide (#108)

Garbage bags or a large sheet of plastic
Liquid dishwashing detergent
Hose or sprinkler

This is great fun for a hot day. Spread out a large sheet of plastic or a few garbage bags which have been cut open. Pour a little bit of liquid dishwashing detergent on the plastic, then turn the hose or sprinkler on it. Your kids will have great fun getting a running start then sliding on the plastic. This works great at the foot of a slide, or on a gentle slope.

Mud Pie (#109)

Sand
Dirt
Water
Bucket
Cake pan or pie plate
Grass or flower petals for decoration

Make some really good mud for your child to play with. Hand-mix sand, clean dirt and water in a large bucket. It's best if you keep the mud really thick. Give your child a cake pan or pie plate and let him go to it. Decorate with grass or flower petals and bake in the sun.

Kickball (#110)

All the balls you can find

Gather together all the balls you can find in your house: tennis, soccer, basketball, beachball, etc. Line them up one foot apart and have your child kick each one. See which one is the easiest to kick, which one goes the farthest, which one goes the highest, etc.

Water Fight (#111)

Water balloons, water pistols, garden hose,
    or tub of water and plastic containers

Using water balloons, water pistols, a garden hose, or a big tub or pool of water and some plastic containers, have a water fight with your child. Invite some of your child's friends over for the fun, and serve popsicles or ice cream cones afterwards.

Nature Walk (#112)

Notebook
Pen or pencil

Take a nature walk with your child. Try to notice as many different types of trees, bugs and birds as you can. Keep a list of what you see. Write down any questions that he asks; look up the answers on your next trip to the library.

Berry Picking (#113)

Sunscreen
Sunhat
Bagged lunch
Juice
Books

Every child should pick berries at least once in his life! Strawberries are the easiest for kids as they are low to the ground, easy to see, and have no thorns. Find a farm that allows you to pick your own fruit. Go early in the day before it gets too hot, and don't forget the sunscreen and a sunhat. Most preschoolers won't last more than half an hour at this, so take lunch, juice and some books for your child to enjoy in the shade when he tires. At home, have your child help you wash and hull the berries. Homemade jam is a marvellous project if you are feeling ambitious.

Measuring Magic (#114)

Measuring cups and spoons
Bowls or small containers
Water, sand or mud

Give your child an assortment of cups, spoons, bowls and other containers and let her play outdoors with water, sand or mud.

Mining for Gold (#115)

Small rocks
Gold or silver spray paint

Spray some small rocks with gold or silver spray paint to resemble gold or silver nuggets. Bury them in the dirt in your yard, or in the sandbox, and have your child dig for buried treasure with their shovels. Turn this into a treasure hunt by making a map for older children to follow.

ON THE MOVE

*"I suppose there must be in every mother's life the inevitable moment
when she has to take two small children shopping in one big store."*
                                                          Shirley Jackson

Children just naturally have the desire and energy to play all the time, but
there are times when your child will just have to sit. It may be a long ride
in the car, or at the doctor's, dentist's or hairdresser's, or while you wait for
your meal to arrive in a restaurant. Consider providing your child with her
very own take-along *Busy Bag* (see Chapter 1). No matter where you are or
what you are doing, being prepared with quick, easy activities that require a
minimum of props will keep a cranky child calm, and a crazy parent sane.

Add-On Stories (#116)

This is a good game for the dinner table, or riding in the car. One person
starts a story and each person takes a turn continuing it. You may want to
have each person add a sentence, or choose a "pointer" to conduct the story.
The pointer decides who goes next and can stop a person at any time, even
in mid-sentence.

Fun with Words (#117)

Ask your child to tell you what certain words mean to her. Pick out everyday
words that she has likely heard before. Some suggestions to start you off;
concrete, marriage, retire, divorce, bachelor, anniversary, occasion, special,
obedient, country. You may be surprised to find that some of the words in his
own vocabulary are something of a mystery. Some of the answers you get
will be priceless; write them down for posterity!

What Am I? (#118)

Make up riddles about animals, objects or people for your child to solve. For
an elephant you could say "I am very large; I have a long trunk; I live in
Africa. What am I?". A firetruck could be "I am big and red; I have a loud
siren; I help put out fires. What am I?". Describe people by what they do
(doctor, nurse, policeman), or friends and family by how they look (tall,
wears glasses, long hair).

Beep (#119)

Read or recite a familiar story, song or rhyme to your child. Substitute wrong words or names in obvious places and have your child listen for the incorrect words and say "Beep!" when she hears one: "Old MacDonald had a *car* ...", or "Mary had a little *dog* ...", etc.

Silly Questions (#120)

Ask your child silly questions that will help her learn to use her imagination and make choices, eg. "Would you rather be a bird or a cow? Why?", Would you rather be a table or a chair? Why?".

Something Blue (#121)

Look around you as you wait in a doctor's office, restaurant, or as you drive in the car. Have your child name five things that are blue, red, yellow, etc.

Magnet Fun (#122)

Refrigerator magnets, magnet-backed letters and number
Cookie sheet or cake pan

This one will help keep your little ones busy in the car when going on a longer trip. Bring along all the magnetic-backed toys you can find, including fridge magnets, magnet-backed letters, numbers, etc. Your child can use the magnets to spell words or create pictures on the cookie sheet or cake pan.

Felt Doll (#123)

Felt
Pen or marker
Cardboard
Glue
Scissors
Scraps of yarn and fabric

Draw the shape of a person on a square of felt. The person should have clearly defined arms and legs, with the arms held away from the body. Glue the felt to a piece of cardboard and cut out the doll. Glue on yarn for hair, and draw a face with a marker. To make clothing for the doll, use a marker to trace around the body on scraps of fabric. Cut out the clothes and dress the doll; the cloth will stick to the doll's felt body. Store the doll and clothes in a shoebox and take with you on a long car ride.

Guessing Bag (#124)

Pillowcase or drawstring bag
Small, unbreakable household objects

Place a variety of small, unbreakable household objects inside a bag and allow your child to feel the objects and guess what they are.

Edible Necklace (#125)

Shoestring licorice
Cereal or crackers with holes in the middle

Use a piece of shoestring licorice (or a plain piece of string) and some cereal or crackers with holes in them. Tie a knot at one end of the licorice, show your child how to thread the cereal on, and then tie both ends together into a knot. The end result will amuse your child for quite some time; in the grocery store she can eat one piece each time you put something in the cart, or in the car she can eat one piece each time she sees a dog or a red car.

Portable Flannel Board (#126)

Shoe box
Felt
Scissors

Cover the top of a shoe box with felt to make a small flannel board. Cut various colours of flannel into different sizes and shapes, such as animals, cars, people, circles, squares, or triangles, or try letters and numbers if you feel ambitious. Stores the pieces in the box and take it along on your next car trip. Your child can form designs or words on the top of the shoe box using the pieces you have cut out.

6.

Reading, Writing, 'rithmetic & More

" ... children must be ready to learn from the first day of school. And of course, preparing children for school is a historic responsibility of parents."

George Bush

Parents have few responsibilities more important or more rewarding than helping their child to learn. As a parent, you are your child's first and most important teacher. Children generally learn what adults around them value, and you can use your daily activities to informally teach them about reading, math, geography and science. Children are naturally curious, and there is much you can do to advance their knowledge in these academic areas. The activities that follow will assist you in providing opportunities for your child to understand the connection between academic knowledge and the skills you use every day at home and at work.

READING READINESS

During the preschool years, children develop at an extraordinary rate. Each day's experiences, however familiar to adults, can be fresh and exciting for curious preschoolers. Although your child's incessant curiosity might be aggravating, especially at the end of a long day, it provides an opportunity for you to help him connect daily experiences with words. Tying language to the world your child knows allows him to go beyond that world to explore new ideas. Not only are there abundant opportunities for a parent to help children develop language, but these opportunities often occur naturally and easily.

While connecting experience to language is an important foundation for learning to read, giving your child direct contact with books is equally important. When you read to your children, they almost automatically learn about written language. They learn that the words in a particular written story are always in the same order and on the same page. They may also learn that print goes from left to right and that there are spaces between words. *Appendix B* on page 150 provides a list of some of the best read-aloud books for young children.

In addition, while reading with your child, you will often have opportunities to answer his questions about the names and sounds of letters and can easily point them out. Preschoolers are very observant and often focus on company trademarks and logos that include or resemble letters of the alphabet. For example, the golden arches at McDonald's look like an M; pointing that out may be an easy way to begin. Television programs like Sesame Street also may help your child learn letters and the sounds they represent. Try to watch these shows with your child so that you can talk to him about the letters on the screen and point out all the other places those letters appear.

Research has shown that children who enter school already knowing the names and sounds of letters do better in learning to read. The following activities will help your preschooler learn to identify letters, sounds and words.

Alphabet Playdough (#127)

Playdough or modelling clay (see Chapter 2)

Help your child form letters out of playdough or modelling clay. Have him close his eyes, feel a letter and try to identify it by shape. A tasty variation, make up some *Alphabet Cookie* dough (see Chapter 4) and bake your alphabet!

Alphabet Match-Up (#128)

Clothespins
Paper
Tape
Pen or marker
Old magazines
Scissors

Write the letters of the alphabet on small pieces of paper and tape to clothespins, or print the letter right on the clothespin itself. Cut out pictures, one for each letter of the alphabet, from magazines and have your child match the clothespin letter to the beginning sound of the object in the picture. Clip the clothespin onto the picture.

Alphabet Puzzle (#129)

Index cards
Pen or markers
Scissors

Print a capital letter on the left side of an index card, the corresponding lowercase letter on the right. Cut each card into two parts with different patterns. Mix up the puzzle pieces and have your child put them together again.

Dictionary Zoo (#130)

Small notebook or loose sheets of paper
Crayons or markers
Old magazines
Scissors
Glue

This is a good rainy day project that can be worked on and finished over time. Help your child print a letter of the alphabet on each page of a small notebook, or use loose sheets of plain or coloured paper. Have your child draw a picture of an animal that begins with that letter, or cut animal pictures from old magazines and glue them onto each page.

Alphabet Book (#131)

Small notebook or loose sheets of paper
Crayons or markers
Old magazines
Scissors
Glue
Photos of friends and family (optional)

This is a long-term project that is great for rainy afternoons. Help your child print a letter of the alphabet on each page of a small notebook, or use loose sheets of plain or coloured paper. Your child can draw a picture of something that begins with that letter, cut pictures from old magazines and glue them onto each page, or use photographs of friends and family members.

Find the Letter (#132)

Paper
Scissors
Pen or marker
Coffee mugs or tea cups (3)

Cut out circles of paper small enough to hide beneath a tea or coffee cup. Write different letters on each circle. Place three tea or coffee cups on the table and hide a paper circle under only one of them. Have your child guess where the letter is and say what the letter is when he finds it. Let him take turns hiding a different circle for you to find.

What Is It? (#133)

Paper
Pen, marker or crayon

Draw a dot-to-dot outline of a picture such as a house, one that will be simple enough for your child to connect the dots. (Try tracing some pictures from your child's colouring books.) Starting with the letter A, place each letter of the alphabet at consecutive dots and have your child connect the dots by identifying each letter.

X's and O's (#134)

Paper
Pen, marker or crayons

Print one letter at the top and center of a sheet of paper. Below this, write many letters of the alphabet in no particular pattern, spreading them over the sheet of paper. Have your child circle the letters that match the one printed at the top. Have him place an "X" over the ones that do not match. For a variation, use pictures cut from old magazines and have your child identify the pictures that begin with the letter you have written.

Give Me An "A" (#135)

Index cards or paper
Pen or marker
Tape

Print the letters of the alphabet on index cards and tape several cards on the windows or around the house. Tell your child what each letter is, then have him bring you the letter you ask for. Or show your child an object, such as an apple, and have him bring you the letter "A". You can also play this by mixing up the cards on a table and having your child pick out the specified letters. For younger children, use fewer cards at a time.

Word Recognition   (#136)

Index cards
Pen or marker
Old magazines
Photographs (optional)
Scissors
Glue

Once your child can recognize the letters of the alphabet, you may want to start practicing simple word recognition. On one set of index cards, write some simple words to start, such as cat, dog or bird. On another set draw or cut out from magazines pictures of these words. Lay all the cards on the table, face up, and have your child match each word to the corresponding picture.

Try name recognition by using photographs of your child, his siblings, friends, relatives, Mommy, Daddy, etc. Write the name of each person on an index card and have your child match the photo to the appropriate name.

Raisin Play (#137)

Toothpicks
Raisins
Paper
Pen, crayon or marker

Put toothpicks into raisins for your child. On a piece of paper, draw letters and shapes that correspond to the size of the toothpick. Have your child connect toothpicks to create each letter or shape. You may not need to draw the letters or shapes for older children.

Connect the Dots (#138)

Paper
Pen or marker
Crayon

Draw a large dot-to-dot outline of your child's name on paper. Have him use a crayon to connect the dots to spell his name.

My Name (#139)

Paper
Pen or marker
Clear contact paper
Crayon or marker
Damp cloth

Help your child learn to print his name. Draw two parallel solid lines with a broken line in the middle. Print your child's name on the lines and cover with clear contact paper. Using a crayon or marker, he can trace over his name and wipe it off when finished.

Name Game (#140)

Index cards
Pen or marker

Print each letter in your child's name on an index card. Lay them out for your child in the order they go in to spell his name. Mix them up and have him try to put them back in the proper order.

I See A-B-C (#141)

While on a walk, in the car, or at the grocery store, look for objects beginning with each letter of the alphabet.

MATHEMATICS

Most children enter school with the skills they need to succeed in math. They are curious about quantities, patterns, and shapes. In many respects, they are natural problem solvers. You can help build your child's math confidence without being an expert yourself. You can instill an interest in math in your child by doing math together -- by asking questions that evoke thinking in terms of numbers and amounts and playing games that deal with such things as logic, reason, estimation, direction, classification, and time. Teach your child that math is a part of the real world. Shopping, travelling, gardening, meal planning, cooking, eating, even laundry are all opportunities that allow you to apply math to your daily routine. Use the following activities as a fun way to help your child develop his math skills.

Counting (#142)

Give your child household counting assignments. Have him count all the doorknobs in the house, or all the cans in the kitchen cupboard, or all the knives, forks and spoons in the silverware drawer. You can adapt this game for outside by counting cars as you go for a walk, birds that fly by as you play on the swings, etc.

Food Count (#143)

Empty egg carton
Pen or marker
Small food items (raisins, cereal, chocolate chips, candies)

Number the individual sections of an egg carton from 1 to 12. Have your child count out each amount using the food pieces, and fill the numbered section with the correct number of items. Once the sections are filled, work in reverse, having your child identify each number, count the pieces, then eat them!

Number Fun (#144)

Index cards or small pieces of paper
Pen or marker
Tape

Write the numbers 1 through 10 on index cards or separate sheets of paper. Tape them on the windows around your house and ask your chld to bring you a particular number. When he has mastered this, have him count a certain object, eg. number of plates on the table, and bring you the card with the correct number.

Thirty Days Has September (#145)

Teach your child this rhyme about the number of days in each month:

Thirty days has September,
April, June and November.
All the rest have thirty-one,
Except February, which has twenty-
*   eight days clear,*
And twenty-nine each leap year.

Number Match-Up (#146)

Index cards
Pen or marker
Old magazines (optional)
Scissors (optional)
Glue (optional)

Make up two sets of index cards; on one set write numbers from one to ten, or as high as you want. On the other set, draw (or cut out from magazines) pictures of objects that correspond to the numbers on the first set. Lay all the cards on the table, face up, and have your child match each numbered card to the card with the corresponding number of objects.

I Spy (#147)

This word game can help develop your child's shape and colour recognition skills. As you drive or walk along, say "I spy with my little eye something that is orange", or "... something that is square". Your child will have fun guessing what it is you see. Take turns and try guessing what your child sees.

One, Two, Buckle My Shoe (#148)

This rhyme will help your child's counting skills. Try showing him objects in groups of one, two, three, etc., as you recite the rhyme together.

One, two, buckle my shoe;
Three, four, close the door;
Five, six, pick up sticks;
Seven, eight, lay them straight;
Nine, ten, a big fat hen.

Telling Time (#149)

Coloured construction paper
Scissors
Paper plate
Paper fastener
Crayon, pen or marker

In these days of digital everything, your child may not see many conventional clocks, but telling time the "old way" is still a skill he should learn. Make a play clock with your child that he can use to practice telling time. Cut big and little hands out of coloured construction paper and attach to a paper plate with a paper fastener. Using a crayon, pen or marker, number the clock appropriately. Your child can move the hands around the clock and tell the time.

Glitter Shapes (#150)

Construction paper
Glue
Glitter or *Colourful Creative Salt*

Draw different shapes with glue on paper: square, rectangle, triangle, heart, circle, oval, star. Have your child sprinkle glitter (or *Colourful Creative Salt,* Chapter 2) over the shapes. Shake off the extra glitter and practice the names of each shape.

Shape Match-Up (#151)

Coloured construction paper
White construction paper
Pen or marker
Scissors

Cut basic shapes out of a piece of coloured construction paper: circle, square, rectangle, triangle, heart, etc. Trace all of the shapes onto a piece of white construction paper. Have your child match the coloured shapes to those drawn on the white paper.

What's Different? (#152)

Various household objects

Give your child a group of objects, maybe three or four, that are related in some way: eating utensils, things to draw with, books, fruit, etc. Add one item that doesn't fit in and have your child identify it and tell you why it doesn't belong.

Cards (#153)

Deck of playing cards

Using a deck of playing cards, place one red card and one black card on the table or floor. Give your child a small stack of cards and have him practice sorting them into either the red pile or the black pile. You can also do this with each of the four suits or with the numbers on the cards.

GEOGRAPHY

Geography is the study of the Earth, divided into five major themes: *location* ("where is it?"); *place* (what makes a place special, both physically and culturally); *interaction* (between people and the environment); *movement* (of people, products and information); and *regions* (areas defined by distinctive characteristics). Geography is a way of thinking, of asking questions, of observing and appreciating the world around us.

You can help your child develop an interest in geography by providing interesting activities for him, and by prompting him to ask questions about his surroundings. To help you think geographically, and to help your child build precise mental images, try to use basic geographical terms whenever possible, i.e. west or north, climate, highway, river and desert. Expose your child to lots of maps and let him see you using maps regularly.

The following activities are only a few examples of the many ways children learn geography. They are informal and easy to do, and are designed to help you find ways to include geographic thinking in your child's early experiences.

Play City (#154)

Markers
Large sheet of paper

Using markers on a large sheet of paper, draw an imaginary city big enough for your child's cars and trucks. Be sure to include some of the landmarks that your child is familiar with: bank, grocery store, gas station, park, hospital, school, post office, train tracks, etc. Tape the finished city to the floor so that your child can travel around the city with his cars, trucks, and fire engines. For a more permanent city, use paints on strong cardboard or wood. Glue on milk cartons or small boxes for buildings. For a variation, try making an imaginary airport or farm.

North, South, East, West (#155)

Small toy, book, or household object

Show your children north, south, east and west by using your home as a reference point. If your child's bedroom faces east, point out the sun rising in the morning. Show the sunset through a window facing west. Once your child has his directional bearings, hide a small toy or household object somewhere in the house. Give directions to its location: "two steps to the north, three steps west ..."

Where Do We Live? (#156)

Map of your city, town or neighbourhood

Look for your city, town or neighbourhood on a map. Point out where your house is, where relatives and best friends live. Find the school your child will attend and show your child its location in relation to your house and street. Find the nearest park, lake, mountain or other cultural or physical feature on the map and talk about how these features affect your life. Living near the ocean may make your climate moderate, prairies may provide an open path for high winds, and mountains may block some weather fronts.

Draw a Map (#157)

Paper
Pens or markers

Help your child draw a simple map of his neighbourhood. Include familiar and personal landmarks on his map: the mailbox, the store, the playground, his friend's house, the fire station. Take this map with you on your walks and point out the landmarks as you go. On your walk, collect natural materials such as acorns and leaves to use for an art project. At home, map the location where you found these items. You can also draw maps of your yard, your house, or his bedroom.

Treasure Hunt (#158)

Paper
Pens or markers
Small toys or other treats

Have a treasure hunt in the park, on the beach, in your backyard or in your house. Draw a map that leads to the treasure, which can be several small toys, cars, or other items.

My Neighbourhood (#159)

Take a walk around your neighbourhood and look at what makes it unique. Point out differences from and similarities to other places. Can your child distinguish various types of homes and shops? Look at the buildings and talk about their uses. Are there features built to conform with the weather or topography? Do the shapes of some buildings indicate how they were used in the past or how they are used now? These observations help children understand the character of a place.

People, Places and Things (#160)

Maps

Go around your house and look at where everything comes from. Look at the labels of the clothes you wear and think of where your food comes from. Why do bananas come from Central America? Why does the milk come from the local dairy? Maybe your climate is too cold for bananas, and the milk is too perishable to travel far. Talk about where your ancestors came from, and use a map to find the countries. Show your child on a map where family and friends live now.

Litter Patrol (#161)

Disposing of waste is a problem with a geographic dimension.

Bag for litter
Gloves
Stick with pointed end

Go on a neighbourhood litter patrol with your child. You may want to wear gloves and use a stick with a pointed end to pick up the litter. Talk about litter, garbage and recycling and how we control our surroundings.

Coin & Stamp Collecting (#162)

Coins and stamps from your own and other countries
Small box, notebook, or coin and stamp collecting books
Glue and tape

Start your preschooler on a coin and stamp collection. Ask friends and family travelling abroad to collect coins for you. Compare the coins and see what information they contain about the country. Stamps tell many different things about a country, from its political leadership to native bird life. Show your child how to remove the stamps from your incoming mail by soaking them in a small amount of warm water. Give him special notebooks to glue the stamps and tape the coins into, or save them in a small box.

Cloud Watching (#163)

Climate is an important part of a region's geographic character. On a warm and lazy afternoon, lay down in the grass with your child and watch the clouds drifting in the sky. Talk about how the clouds are formed (water which has evaporated from the earth condenses into small droplets) and what happens when clouds touch the earth (fog). Help him pick out shapes and afterwards have him draw what he saw.

Language Play (#164)

Learn simple words in different languages. Teach your child to count to 10 in other languages, and simple words like "hello", "goodbye", and "thank you". Have a theme day when you locate a country on the map and talk about the unique aspects of its location. Talk about the language spoken there and if possible, learn several words in that language. Serve a special lunch or snack that originated in that country.

BASIC BOTANY

Your child's early efforts at gardening may be clumsy, but he will be learning the basics of botany, getting dirty, and having fun all at the same time. You can teach your child how seeds develop into four basic parts: the roots, the stems, the leaves and the flower that in turn fruits with new seed. He will learn that plants eat minerals through their roots, that earthworms fertilize the soil and aereate it so the roots can breathe better. Teach him how the leaves inhale carbon dioxide and exhale oxygen, which is why nature needs a balance between animals and plants. Explain that plants are the only living things that make their own food, chlorophyll.

Use the following activities to teach your child, in an informal and fun way, the basic principles of botany.

Growing Plants (#165)

>Seeds
>Shallow dish of water
>Planters
>Potting soil

Your preschooler will be fascinated to see how plants grow from seeds or cuttings. Soak seeds such as orange, apple, grapefruit, lemon or lime seeds in water for a day or two. Fill several planters with potting soil and place three or four seeds in each one about 1/2" deep. Water and place in a sunny spot and watch for the green shoots to grow. You can try plantings seeds in a pattern or shape: a letter, number, square or circle.

Garlic Clove   (#166)

Garlic clove
Potting soil
Small pot

Plant an unpeeled garlic clove in potting soil, pointed ends up. Cover completely, water every few days, and keep in the sun.

Lima Bean Sprouts   (#167)

Lima beans
Shallow dish
Water

Put lima beans in a dish and fill with water. Place the dish in a sunny window and watch how they change daily.

Sweet Potato Vine   (#168)

Sweet potato
Toothpicks
Glass of water
String

To start a vine, stick three toothpicks in the sides of an old sweet potato. Set it in a glass of water with the toothpicks resting on the rim of the glass. The water should just cover the tip of the sweet potato. Put the glass in a place where the vine will get filtered sunlight. Pin up some strings so it can climb.

Carrots & Beets   (#169)

Carrots or beets
Shallow dish of water
Small pot
Potting soil

Cut two inches off the top of a carrot or beet. Set cut side down in a dish with 1/2" of water. Change the water often. When roots appear plant your carrot or beet, cut side down, in a pot of moist soil. Set it in a sunny window and keep it wet.

Avocado Tree (#170)

Avocado seed
5" pot
Potting soil

Dry the avocado seed for a couple of days, then peel the papery brown skin off. Plant about two-thirds down in a pot of soil, base down, leaving the pointed tip exposed until the seed germinates (30 to 90 days). You can keep this in the sun, or well-watered in a dark cupboard for a stronger root system. When it starts to grow, pinch off the new growth and it will grow into a lush, bushy tree.

Flower Tinting (#171)

Clear glass or vase
Water
Food colouring
White carnation or daisy

This is a good activity to show your child how plants drink water through their stalks, and where the water goes. Fill a clear glass or vase halfway with water and add enough food colouring to tint the water a bright colour. Add a white carnation or daisy and watch the flower change colour over the next few hours.

7.

Music, Dance & Drama

"The events of childhood do not pass, but repeat themselves like seasons of the year."

Eleanor Farjeon

Music, dance and drama are an essential part of our children's general education. Through the study of music, dance and drama, children acquire knowledge, skills and attitudes that influence them throughout their lives. In addition to learning music for its own sake, children who participate in music learn coordination, goal-setting, concentration and cooperation. Dance activities also offer many benefits for children, encouraging mental and emotional development while enhancing motor skills. Drama involves mind, body and imagination, and is essential to a child's full development.

This chapter provides simple ideas that will help you to stimulate your child's development in these three areas. The following activities will cultivate your child's sense of rhythm, allow your child to experience movement as it relates to music and rhythm, and encourage your child in creative play.

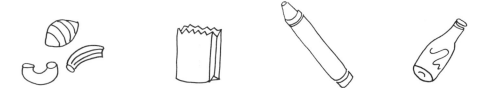

MUSIC & RHYTHM

As a parent, you can encourage your child's love of music and nurture her musical talents in a number of ways: by listening to good music programs and recordings together, by attending musical events and making music as a family, and by praising children for their musical activities and accomplishments. As a result of music-listening and music-making experiences, children can become better listeners and develop musical intelligence.

Listening to music, moving to music and playing musical games are the best musical activities for small children. The following ideas will help you begin to develop your child's sense of music and rhythm.

Tambourine (#172)

Corn kernels, dried beans, small pasta, cereal, etc.
Two paper plates
Glue or staples
Ribbon
Crayons, markers, stickers for decoration

Place corns, beans, pasta or cereal inside two paper plates and glue or staple the rims of the plates together. When the glue is dry, punch holes around the rims and lace ribbon through the holes. Let your child decorate with crayons, markers, stickers, etc.

Button Tap (#173)

Large buttons with two holes
Elastic bands
Empty cooking pots

Insert the looped ends of an elastic band into the two holes of a large button. Bring the looped ends together and slide onto your child's finger. Put a few of these on each hand and let your child tap out some music on an upside down pot.

Rhythm Blocks (#174)

Two 4" pieces of a two-by-four piece of wood

Your child can use two pieces of wood as rhythm blocks, banging them together in time to a rhythmic beat.

Shakers (#175)

Plastic medicine bottles in various sizes, or soap bottles,
   or small aluminum pie or tart pans
Corn, rice, dried beans, pennies, etc.

Using a collection of different sizes of plastic medicine bottles, soap bottles, or small aluminum pie or tart pans, partially fill each with anything that will create noise; corn, rice, dried beans, pennies, etc. Use a variety of items for filling as they each make a different sound.

Sandpaper Blocks (#176)

Two 4" pieces of a two-by-four piece of wood
Sandpaper

Glue sandpaper onto the wood and rub together for an interesting sound.

Pie Plate Tambourine (#177)

Aluminum pie plate
Ice pick
6-8 flattened bottle caps
String

Using an ice pick, an adult should make six to eight holes around the edge of an aluminum pic plate, and one hole in the center of the same number of flattened bottle caps. Let your child pull a piece of string through the bottle cap and the hole in the pie plate, making knots tight enough to hold the bottle cap in place, but allowing enough slack so that the cap can move freely and hit the pie plate when shaken. Attach all the caps in this way; shake to play.

Coffee Can Drum (#178)

Empty coffee can with two plastic lids
Contact paper or your child'sartwork
Glue
Sharpened pencil
Empty thread spool

You can create a drum for your child by cutting the bottom out of a coffee can and covering the can with contact paper (or let your child draw a picture on some paper and glue around the can). Glue plastic lids on each end of the can. Create a drumstick by gluing the sharpened end of a pencil into the hole of an empty thread spool.

For a variation, an empty paper towel roll and an empty oatmeal box will make a soft but authentic drum for your preschooler.

Milk Carton Guitar (#179)

Cardboard milk carton (two litre size)
Tape
Yardstick
Saw
45" length of nylon fishing line

This will make a guitar that your child can really play. Tape shut the top of a clean, empty milk carton. Cut vertical slits, big enough to slip the yardstick through, in two sides of the carton, two-thirds up from the bottom. Cut a notch about 1/2" deep near each end of the yardstick and insert through the carton. Position the carton near the center of the yardstick. Make a loop in one end of the length of fishing line and slip it over the notch on the top of the yardstick. Pull the line over the top of the carton and loop it around the notch at the other end of the yardstick. Tie securely and pull the carton to one end of the yardstick. To play the guitar, strum the string near the top edge of the milk carton with one hand. Pinch the string to the yardstick with the other to change pitches.

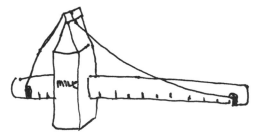

Noise Blower (#180)

Empty toilet paper tube
Wax paper
Elastic band
Crayons, markers, stickers, fabric, etc., for decoration

To turn a cardboard toilet paper tube into a fun noisemaker, cover one end with a piece of wax paper using an elastic band to hold the wax paper in place. Blow and hum into the uncovered end to make a vibrating sound. An older child can make this for herself, decorating the tube with crayons, markers, stickers, or scraps of ribbon, fabric or construction paper.

Tom Toms (#181)

Small pop-top juice cans
Popcorn
Tape

Fill small, empty, pop-top juice cans with a small amount of unpopped popcorn. Tape the hole closed and shake, shake, shake.

MOVEMENT & DANCE

For young children, dance offers avenues for exploration, discovery and the development of natural instincts for movement. Dance has many physical benefits, among them increased flexibility, improved circulation, development of tone and muscles, and improved posture, balance and coordination. But although dance can be great exercise, it is primarily an artistic expression of mind and body. Dancing offers opportunities to express thoughts and feelings and to understand other's thoughts and feelings.

As a parent, you can offer your child early exposure to the art of dance through movement activities such as those that follow.

Let's Pretend (#182)

Have your child tell a story by acting it out with body movements, or ask her to move with different types of walks (downhill, on parade, stiff, up stairs) or pretend to use different kinds of vehicles (bicycle, skateboard, car, horse, etc.). This will provide your child with the opportunity to explore and invent movement.

Moving Questions (#183)

Ask your child questions like "How many ways can you balance yourself besides standing?", and "How many different ways can you move your head (arms, leg, upper body)?". Questions like these will help your child become aware of her body and its relationship to other people and the environment.

Exercise Class (#184)

Pretend to have an exercise class in your living room. You can dress in exercise wear if you like, and take turns being the "instructor". Include both locomotor movements (walking, running, jumping, skipping, etc.) and non-locomotor movements (bending, stretching, twisting, swinging, etc.). Varying the size, level and direction of these basics allows your child to discover a large number of movements which can be combined to form basic dance steps. You can also make a point of including these movements in other games you play, such as *Simon Says* or *Follow the Leader* (Chapter 3).

Music & Movement (#185)

> Homemade rhythm instruments, or musical instruments such as piano, guitar, etc., or recorded music

The goal of this activity is to have your child experience movement as it relates to music or rhythm. Play different types of music and have your child physically express how the music makes her feel: run for fast music, tiptoe for soft music, hop and bounce for happy music, march for a parade tune, etc. You can also tap out a rhythmic beat and encourage your child to clap or hop in time to the beat.

Hokey Pokey (#186)

This is a good song to stress body movement. Do the actions as the song says. To do the Hokey Pokey, point your hands upwards at shoulder height and shake them while you wiggle your body from side to side.

> *You put your left hand in,*
> *You put your left hand out.*
> *You put your left hand in,*
> *And you shake it all about.*
> *You do the Hokey Pokey and*
> *You turn yourself around.*
> *That's what it's all about.*

Chorus:
> *You do the Hokey Pokey* (all join hands and move into the circle, raising arms above your head)
> *You do the Hokey Pokey* (lower arms as you move out)
> *You do the Hokey Pokey* (move into the circle and raise arms again)
> *That's what it's all about* (clapping to the beat).

> *You put your right hand in ...*
> *You put your left foot in ...*
> *You put your right foot in ...*
> *You put your head in ...*
> *You put your whole self in ...*

Looby Loo (#187)

For this traditional song, hold hands and skip in a circle. Do the actions as
the song says.

Chorus:
> *Here we go looby loo,*
> *Here we go looby light.*
> *Here we go looby loo,*
> *All on a Saturday night.*

> *You put your right hand in,*
> *You take your right hand out.*
> *You give your hand a shake, shake, shake,*
> *And turn yourself about. Oh...* (chorus)

> *You put your left hand in ...*
> *You put your right foot in ...*
> *You put your left foot in ...*
> *You put your right arm in ...*
> *You put your left arm in ...*
> *You put your right leg in ...*
> *You put your left leg in ...*
> *You put your head in ...*
> *You put your whole self in ...*

DRAMATIC PLAY

Children of all ages love to pretend. As toddlers, they first enter the world of
make-believe by engaging in activities they see around them and by putting
themselves in the place of others. This activity involves mind, body and
imagination. It is a child's rehearsal for life and is essential to a child's full
development.

As children grow older, their play develops more structure. They act out
favourite stories, create original situations from life experiences, and imagine
themselves in fantasy worlds where anything is possible. If they are
encouraged in this kind of play at home, they become ready for creative
drama by the time they enter primary school. As essential as dramatic play
is to a child's healthy development, creative drama is an art form, a
socializing activity and a means of learning.

The following activities will encourage your child's dramatic play.

Tickle Trunk (#188)

Empty trunk or large box
Dress-up clothes and props

You can encourage your child's dramatic play by setting up a Tickle Trunk full of props for her. Set aside a trunk or box and fill it with grown-up clothes, shoes, hats, scarves, gloves and costume jewellery to use for "dress-ups". Old bridesmaid dresses are great, as are Hawaiian shirts, nightgowns, baseball hats, wigs, boots, slippers and purses. Great items can be found at garage sales or the local thrift shop. A tickle trunk will be an invaluable part of your child's play and can be added to for years.

Hospital (#189)

Pillows
Blankets
White clothes for uniforms
Thermometer
Bandages
Medicine spoon
Sling
Stuffed animals

Using friends, stuffed animals or cooperative parents for patients, help your child set up a hospital or doctor's office. Lay pillows and blankets in a corner of the room. Give the "nurse" or "doctor" white clothing for her uniform. Show her how to take temperatures, bandage arms and legs and give medicine. Make a sling from a flat cloth diaper or other piece of material folded into a triangle. Take turns playing the part of doctor, nurse, patient and visitors.

Barber Shop (#190)

Brushes
Combs
Empty hair spray bottle
Popsicle stick or old credit card
Shaving cream
Towel

Help your child set up a pretend barber shop. Give her brushes, combs, an empty hair spray bottle filled with water, and shaving cream. A wooden popsicle stick or old credit card can be used as a razor. Take turns being the barber.

Beauty Salon (#191)

Brushes
Curlers
Hair bows
Empty hair spray bottle
Towel
Nail polish (optional)

Give your child brushes, curlers, hair bows, and an empty hair spray bottle filled with water to use in her beauty salon. Use friends, siblings or parents for clients, and take turns being the hairdresser. Help her put polish on her fingers and toes as a special treat.

Grocery Store (#192)

Empty food boxes and containers
Old purse or wallet
Play money
Store coupons
Grocery list
Paper grocery bag

Help your child set up a grocery store by saving empty boxes, plastic containers, non-breakable jars, etc. Give her an old purse or wallet containing play money and coins. She can practice her cutting skills by cutting out your unwanted coupons to use in her store. Help her make up a shopping list and give her a bag for her groceries.

Dentist (#193)

Cup with water
Bowl for spitting
Paper napkin
Flashlight
Toothbrush
Small toys for "prizes"

Because water is involved, this game is best played in the kitchen or bathroom. Take turns being the dentist and patient. The dentist tucks the napkin into the patient's collar to protect her shirt, then uses the flashlight to look into her mouth. The dentist may want to brush the patient's teeth, then advise her to rinse her mouth and spit into the bowl. As the patient leaves, be sure the dentist offers her a "prize".

Restaurant (#194)

Tablecloth
Vase with flowers or other centrepiece
Candle (optional)
Menu

Use table linens, flowers (real or other) in a vase, even a candle. Take their coat, show them to their seat, give them a menu and let them order their lunch or dinner. Take turns being the waiter and the customer.

Bakery (#195)

Aprons
Paper lunch bag
Rolling pin
Cookie cutters
Playdough
Prepared cookie dough (optional)

Put on aprons and wear a white paper lunch bag on your head for a baker's hat. With a rolling pin and cookie cutters, bake cookies, pies, and cakes out of play dough. Or using a roll of prepared cookie dough, give your child a plastic knife and have her cut "real" cookies and place them on a cookie sheet for baking.

Post Office (#196)

Unopened "junk mail"
Unused return envelopes from your mail
Inexpensive stationery
Stickers from magazine and record clubs
Paper clips
Bank slips
Rubber stamp and ink pad

Help your child open up a post office of her own. Save unopened junk mail, unused return envelopes from mail you receive, and stickers from magazine and record clubs. You may want to provide her with inexpensive stationery and authentic 1-cent stamps. Use a date stamp or other rubber stamp and inkpad, and bank slips for official looking forms.

8.

Art & Crafts

"The parents exist to teach the child, but also they must learn what the child has to teach them; and the child has a very great deal to teach them."

Arnold Bennett

Art and craft projects provide great opportunity for creative play for your child. Through his work with art and crafts, your child will learn to think creatively while developing skills in drawing, painting, sculpting, designing and crafting. Well-chosen art and craft projects will help your child develop concentration and coordination, as well as organizational and manipulative skills. They will promote a sense of great achievement, and are fun and exciting for children of all ages.

Here are activities you can use to introduce your child to the world of art. Remember that your own attitudes make strong impressions on your child; encourage him to experiment. Art and craft projects are a form of self-expression and your child should know that there is no one right way.

DRAWING

Drawing is probably the first art form your child will experience. It allows your child to express himself creatively while helping in the development of his small muscles and hand-eye coordination. Drawing is simple and it can be done anywhere and at anytime. It is something that most of us do, in some form or another, all our lives.

Give your child a little variety in his drawing tools and materials. Try using pens, pencil crayons, chalk and markers. For drawing paper use construction paper, newspaper, fine sandpaper or cut-open grocery bags in varying sizes. Your child will also enjoy drawing on shapes such as circles, triangles and stars, cut from different types of paper.

Stained Glass Crayons   (#197)

Broken crayon pieces
Muffin tin

This is a good project to get rid of all those broken crayon pieces. Remove any covering paper from the crayons and place the pieces in a well greased muffin tin (or line it with foil). Place the tin in a 400° oven for a few minutes until the crayons have melted. Remove from the oven and cool completely before removing from the tin. If you have mixed the colours, the circles will have a stained glass effect and are great to colour with.

Clothespin Crayons   (#198)

Clothespins
Crayons
Drawing paper

Clip a clothespin around a crayon and encourage your child to draw while holding onto the clothespin instead of the crayon.

Thumbprint Mice   (#199)

Stamp pad
Crayons or markers

Have your child press his thumb on a stamp pad and then press it on a paper. Show your child how to draw a mouse tail and ears on the thumbprint to complete each mouse. Do this several times to make a mouse family. Use your own thumb and perhaps one of an older or younger sibling, then compare the different sizes each makes.

Self-Portraits (#200)

Very large sheet of newsprint or butcher paper
Markers, crayons or paint

Have your child lie down on the floor on the paper. Trace around him, then let him fill in the details with markers, paint or crayons. Try to get him to be as detailed as he can: What is his hair like? What colour are his eyes? What clothes is he wearing? When finished, hang his portrait in his room or on his door where he can admire it.

Colour of Nature (#201)

Plants and flowers collected on a walk
Crayons
Drawing paper

Go on a walk with your child and bring home a variety of plants and flowers, such as grass, leaves, dandelions, etc. Spread them out on a table in your backyard and encourage your child to draw a picture using only crayons in colors that match the items you have collected.

Rainbow Drawing (#202)

Crayons
Tape
Drawing paper

Tape two or more crayons together and have your child draw a picture. If you want to use true rainbow colours you will need violet, indigo, blue, green, yellow, orange and red.

Fruit Rub (#203)

Cardboard
Scissors
Drawing paper
Paper clips
Crayons

Cut a fruit shape such as an apple, orange or banana out of cardboard. Place the cardboard shape between two sheets of paper and clip together with a paper clip. Using an appropriately coloured crayon, rub over the paper lightly and a red apple or yellow banana will appear.

Crayon Rubbings (#204)

Drawing paper
Small textured objects
Crayons

Place plain drawing paper or cut-open grocery bags over textured objects such as leaves, string, doilies, paper clips, fabric, tiles, coins, cardboard shapes or bricks. Rub the side of the crayon on the paper. Shift the paper and use different colours for interesting patterns.

Wet Chalk Drawings (#205)

Coloured chalk
6 Tbsp. sugar
1/4 cup water
Drawing paper

Mix together sugar and water and soak chalk for 10 minutes. Use the wet chalk to draw on white paper, or use white chalk on coloured paper.

Secret Messages (#206)

White crayon or wax candle
Drawing paper
Tempera paints and brush

Using a white crayon or wax candle, write a message or draw a picture on a piece of white paper. Your child can then paint over the paper with tempera paint to see the picture or message.

Resist Drawing (#207)

Construction paper
Crayons
Tempera paint and brush
Varnish (optional)

Have your child scribble or draw with his crayons on a piece of soft construction or other matte paper. Have him press hard, and fill in with plenty of thick colouring. Then have him paint the picture with tempera paints. Since wax repels water, the wax areas will resist the paint and the painting will glow. For a really dramatic effect, use fluorescent crayons and black paint. You can apply a thin coat of varnish over the picture and have it matted and framed if you wish to save it.

Hand Drawings (#208)

Drawing paper
Crayons or markers
Sparkles or small beads
Glue
Nail polish (optional)

Place your child's hands on a piece of drawing paper and trace around them. Using crayons, markers or the real thing, encourage your child to paint on nail polish. Use glue and sparkles or small beads to add rings, watches and other details.

Foot Tracing (#209)

Drawing paper
Pen, crayons or markers
Nail polish (optional)

Have your child stand on a piece of paper while you trace around his feet with a pen or crayon. Then have him trace your feet and compare sizes. Colour the feet and use crayons or markers to add nail polish and funny rings.

Picture a Story (#210)

Drawing paper
Crayons or markers

Have your child draw a series of pictures, about four or five. Have him then dictate a story to go with each picture. You can write it on the bottom of the picture as it is told.

Blindfold Drawing (#211)

Blindfold
Crayons or markers
Drawing paper

Place a blindfold on your child, then have him draw on paper with crayons or markers. When his drawing is complete, remove the blindfold and take turns looking for hidden shapes or objects in the picture.

Bark Drawing (#212)

Tree bark
Crayons, pens or paint

Collect tree bark while on a walk. At home use crayons, pens or paint to draw pictures on the bark. Talk about how people used tree bark before paper was invented, and how paper comes from trees.

Scribble Drawing (#213)

Drawing paper
Crayons

Show your child how to scribble on a piece of white paper with a crayon, using big circular motions to form loops. Then your child can colour in each loop with a different colour, creating a very pretty and uniquely different design every time.

PAINTING

Painting is a wonderful outlet for a child's creativity. Large pieces of art paper, pots of paint in vivid colours, big art brushes, and a painter's smock will keep your little artist happy on many a rainy afternoon. Provide a good work space, keep supplies handy, and make clean-up part of the project. Work outdoors when you can and let nature provide further inspiration.

The best kind of paint for young children is poster paint, also known as tempera paint. You can buy this at any art store pre-mixed in liquid form, or as a powder which must be mixed with water. You can also make your own poster paint using the recipes in Chapter 2. Children rarely need more than three colours to work with; stick with red, blue and yellow and teach your child how to mix these colours to create others. Tempera blocks are also available and are suitable for projects which require basic painting with brushes. Your child will probably not find them as fun as the slick liquid paints, but they are less expensive, less messy and last a very long time.

Paper can be purchased from an art supply store, but consider some of the following alternatives. Newsprint is a wonderful paper for painting on; roll-ends can be purchased cheaply from a newspaper publisher. Visit your local printer and ask if you can leave a box for a week or two; he may agree to fill it with all kinds of wonderful paper he would otherwise discard. Try fine sandpaper as an alternative art paper for a wonderful effect. For fingerpainting, use the shiny side of freezer paper you can buy at the grocery store. It is much cheaper than special fingerpaint paper and works just as well.

String up a line in the laundry room or kitchen that can be used to hang paintings while they dry. Wet artwork can be attached to the line with clothespins. When dry, be sure to display your child's paintings prominently. And think of creative uses for some of his work; a lot of the painting projects that follow make wonderful giftwrap or greeting cards.

Starch Painting (#214)

Liquid starch
Liquid detergent
Powdered tempera paint

Mix a small amount of detergent with liquid starch and put on a painting surface such as a table top, paper or plastic cloth. Sprinkle tempera paint over the starch and allow your child to experiment with mixing colours.

Dipping (#215)

Paper towel
Bowls of diluted food colouring or strong water colours

Have your child fold a piece of paper towel into a fairly small packet. Have him dip each corner of the packet into bowls of different coloured dye, which can be either diluted food colouring or strong water colours. Unfold the paper towel and hang to dry. You can use different types of paper; the more absorbent the paper, the faster the dye will spread. Dipped rice paper makes a nice gift wrap, but is also fairly expensive.

Fingerpainting (#216)

Fingerpaints
Fingerpaint or butcher paper

Fingerpainting is a wonderfully messy experience that every child should have after about the age of two (younger, if you can stand it!). Unfortunately, it can be a frustrating experience for parents as the amount of work required to set-up and clean-up never seems to merit the five minutes most children will spend at this activity. That said, be prepared for a great big mess and make sure your child wears an art smock. Wet the paper first to allow the paint to slide better, drop a blob of paint on the paper and let your child go to it. Fingerpaints can be commercially bought, or make your own using the recipes in Chapter 2.

String Painting (#217)

Paper
Tempera paint
String or yarn

Drop some paint on a piece of paper and let your child make a design by dragging some string through the paint and around the paper. Try it again by dipping the string in the paint and dragging it across the paper. Use different types and lengths of string and yarn for different effects.

3-D String Painting (#218)

Tempera paint
Liquid starch
Paper
String

For this activity mix paint and liquid starch in equal parts. Dip some string into the paint/starch solution and drop it onto some paper. When the painting dries, the starch will make the string stick to the paper.

Drippy Painting (#219)

Paper
Tempera paint
Eyedropper, spoon or straw

On a big sheet of art paper or a cut-open brown paper bag, have your child drip liquid tempera paints using an eyedropper, spoon or straw. Tip the paper in different directions to make a design. Use another colour and tip again for an interesting result.

Bubble Painting (#220)

Newspaper
Shallow dish
Liquid dishwashing detergent
Tempera paint
Straw
Paper

Cover your work surface with newspaper. Pour 1/4 cup liquid dishwashing detergent into a shallow dish. If using powdered tempera, mix a small amount of water with the paint. Add paint mixture or liquid tempera to the dishwashing liquid until the colour is intense. Place one end of a straw in the mixture and blow until the bubbles are almost billowing over the edge of the pan. Gently place a piece of construction paper or other art paper on top of the bubbles and hold it in place until several bubbles have popped. Continue this process with different colors, blowing more bubbles as needed. To make a unique greeting card, use a piece of construction paper folded in half. When dry, your child can add drawings to the picture and sign his name.

Air Painting (#221)

> Paper
> Tempera paint
> Empty squeeze bottle

Have your child drop some paint on a piece of paper and disperse it by squeezing air onto it with an empty squeeze bottle. He can also do this by blowing on it through a wide plastic tube or straw.

Spray Painting (#222)

> Newspaper
> Paper
> Tempera paint
> Plant sprayer

For this activity you will want to prepare your work area well. Lay down lots of newspaper, and be prepared to offer close supervision. Place some art paper or cut-open brown paper bags on the newspaper. Pour some thin paint into a plant sprayer and let your child spray it onto the paper. Use several different colours, and when the paper is dry you will have some great giftwrap.

Stencil Painting (#223)

> Thin cardboard
> Scissors
> Paper
> Sponge or brush
> Tempera paint

Draw a design, letter or animal shape on thin cardboard. Cut out the shape to make the stencil pattern, and tape the pattern onto the paper you will be painting on. Show your child how to dip a sponge or brush into liquid tempera paint, then fill in the inside of the pattern. When finished, remove the tape and lift off the stencil to see the design.

Paint Blot Art (#224)

Construction paper
Tempera paint
Spoon
Rolling pin

Fold a piece of construction paper in half like a greeting card, then open it up. Using liquid tempera paints and a spoon, have your child drop different colours onto one half of the paper. Fold the paper again with the paint on the inside, and have your child roll a rolling pin over the paper to spread the paint. Open up the paper and have your child use his imagination to decide what the blot looks like. When the paint is dry, fold the paper so that the paint is on the outside. Use as a unique greeting card.

Foot Painting (#225)

Newspaper
Fingerpaint paper
Tempera paint or fingerpaint
Warm, soapy water
Towel
Rubber boots or tennis shoes (optional)

Cover your floor with newspaper, then spread large sheets of butcher or finger paint paper on the newspapers. Pour about 1/4 cup liquid tempera paint or fingerpaint onto the glossy side of the paper. Encourage your bare-footed child to walk, stamp and slide his feet through the paint to make different effects. Have a bucket of warm, soapy water and a towel ready for when the fun is over. For a variation, have your child wear rubber boots or tennis shoes.

Window Stencilling (#226)

Leaves in different shapes and sizes
Masking tape
Sponge
Clothespins
Tempera paint (orange, yellow, red and brown)
Newspaper

On a fall walk with your child, collect several different types and colors of leaves. At home, attach rolled pieces of masking tape to the backsides of the leaves and arrange them on the window in the way you want them to appear in stenciled form. Make sure the leaves are lying flat against the glass. Dip small pieces of sponge clipped onto clothespins into tempera paints in fall colours. Blot on newspaper to absorb excess paint, then lightly dab the sponge around the edge of each leaf. Use a new piece of sponge for each color. When the paint is dry, carefully remove the leaves from the window. The leaf patterns can be easily removed with window cleaner.

Paper Towel Art (#227)

>Paper towel
>Newspaper
>Food colouring

Lay a piece of paper towel over newspaper and show your child how to drop food colouring onto the paper towel. Use different colours to make an interesting design.

Balloon Painting (#228)

>Balloons in various sizes
>Tempera paint
>Paper

Blow up balloons of different sizes and tie the ends. Holding onto the tied end, dip the balloon into tempera paint and blot it onto art paper. The resulting artwork can be displayed on the wall or used as unique gift wrap.

Marble Painting (#229)

>Marbles
>Paper
>Tempera paint

Have your child drop marbles into various colours of paint and roll them across a piece of paper.

Eyedropper Painting (#230)

>Eyedropper
>Tempera paint
>Paper

Using an eyedropper and some liquid tempera paint, show your child how to squeeze the paint into the eyedropper and drop it onto the paper to make a picture. Use different colours if you like, and be sure to put the painting on display when dry.

Straw Painting (#231)

Tempera paint
Paper
Drinking straw

Drop a bit of thin paint on a piece of paper. Give your child a straw and have him blow the paint around. If you like, add a second and third colour. You can also try different types of paper for different effects.

Spatter Painting (#232)

Small objects
Paper
Tempera paint
Paint brush or toothbrush

Have your child collect some interesting objects: elastics, paper clips, yarn, string, leaves, flowers, toothpicks, small shapes cut from paper, etc. Place the objects on a piece of paper and have him spatter paint over them using a paint brush or toothbrush. Remove the objects from the paper and show your child the negative images that appear.

Toothpick Painting (#233)

Toothpicks
Tempera paint
Paper
Glue

Give your child toothpicks to dip into paint and use as a paintbrush. When the paint has dried, he can glue the toothpicks onto his painting for a three-dimensional effect.

Tennis Ball Painting (#234)

Newspaper
Tennis balls
Tempera paint
Paper

This activity is best done outdoors. Spread newspapers on the sidewalk or other firm surface, and place a large sheet of art paper on the ground. Dip tennis balls, a different one for each colour, into tempera paint and bounce them onto the paper for a great painting effect.

Negative Painting (#235)

Textured objects
Glue
Plain white paper
Tempera paint and brush

Gather together a collection of interesting objects such as lace doilies, paper dolls, leaves, or letters, numbers or shapes cut out of cardboard. Have your child place a dab of glue on an object, and stick it to a white piece of paper. He can now paint over the paper and the shape, then remove the shape to see the negative image. You can make a unique greeting card by placing the object on half of the paper before painting and folding when dry.

Paint Pen (#236)

Empty roll-on deodorant bottle
Liquid tempera paint

To make a giant paint pen for your child, pry the top off of a roll-on deodorant bottle. Fill with tempera paint and snap the top back on the bottle. Your child can use this for drawing pictures, practicing his letters and numbers, or for creating abstract designs.

PRINTMAKING

Young children can experience a sense of great accomplishment with printmaking. Not only is it fun, but making prints allows a young child to achieve an attractive reproduction of an object without a great amount of artistic skill or coordination. Through the repetition of an impression, children can develop an appreciation of texture and design.

Printmaking involves making an impression of an object onto paper or another surface. The object to be printed can be covered in paint using a brush, a paint roller, by dipping it into paint, or by pressing it on a print pad.

A print pad can be made by padding up newspaper and soaking it in liquid tempera. Or place a thin sponge into a shallow tray or small bowl and cover with several tablespoons of paint. For some printmaking, a rubber stamp pad can also be used. To cushion the print, place a newspaper under the paper on which the impression is to be made.

Many different types of paper can be used for printing; try newsprint, construction paper, and cut-open brown paper bags. As with the many of the painting projects in this chapter, you can use these printing activities to create some great, environmentally-friendly gift wrap.

Fruit and Vegetable Printing (#237)

> Various fruit and vegetables
> Paring knife
> Print pad or stamp pad
> Paper

Cut different fruits and vegetables and dip in tempera paints or on an ink pad then onto plain or coloured paper. Apples cut in half will leave a "star" design of seeds, while green peppers make a great shamrock design. Cut a potato in half and use a small paring knife to create a relief design: circles, square, hearts, etc. If you make letters, don't forget to carve them backwards so they will print correctly.

Playdough Printing (#238)

> Playdough
> Tools for making a design
> Print pad
> Paper

Roll playdough into a ball and flatten it until it is about 2" thick. On one side of the dough, press in a design using a pencil, bottle cap, cookie cutter, or other cooking utensil. Gently press the clay onto the print pad then onto paper. Repeat using various colours and designs.

Gadget Printing (#239)

> 1/2" softwood cubes or matchboxes
> Small objects in interesting shapes
> Glue
> Print pad or stamp pad
> Paper

Use 1/2" softwood cubes or matchboxes and glue on interesting shapes; matchsticks, string, wood chips, curtain rings, keys, bottle caps, or shapes cut from cardboard. You can make stamps of letters or numbers on wood cubes by drawing the image in reverse, then chipping away the surface except for the shape to be printed. Or use larger objects to make an impression, such as a potato masher, fly swatter, or salt shaker. Press the object onto the print pad or rubber stamp pad and stamp it on the paper, varying colours and objects to create unique designs.

Mesh Printing (#240)

Scissors
Plastic mesh
Small foam ball
Twist-tie
Tempera paint
Shallow tray or dish
Paper

Cut out a small square of plastic mesh, enough to gather around a small foam ball. Secure the ends with a twist-tie. Pour liquid tempera paint into a shallow tray or dish. Dip the mesh ball into the paint, and dab the mesh onto a piece of art paper. Use different colours for a unique effect.

Sponge Printing (#241)

Scissors
Small thick sponges
Clothespins
Print pad
Paper

Cut sponges into various shapes. On the top of each sponge cut two slots for the clothespins to clip into, making each slot about 1cm deep and 2 cm apart. Clip the clothespins onto the top of each sponge to use as a handle. Press the sponge onto the print pad and stamp it onto the paper. Use various shapes and different colours for an interesting effect.

Roller Printing (#242)

Thin foam
Scissors
Glue
Empty toilet paper or paper towel roll
Tempera paint
Shallow pan
Art paper

Cut out some interesting shapes from thin pieces of foam. Stars are nice, or hearts, Christmas trees, etc., depending on the season. Glue the shapes onto empty paper towel or toilet paper rolls. Pour some liquid tempera paint into a shallow pan big enough for the paper roll to fit in. Dip the "roller" into the paint, then roll onto some art paper or a cut-open brown paper bag.

For a variation on this, use a real foam paint roller. At even intervals, tie the roller with string. This will make stripes when dipped in paint and pressed on paper. Or cut chunks out of the roller to make a thick solid pattern with holes in it.

Fingerpaint Prints (#243)

Fingerpaint
Plastic tabletop
Large sheets of paper

Fingerpaint can be commercially bought, or you can make your own using the fingerpaint recipes in Chapter 2. Place a small amount of fingerpaint onto the tabletop and have your child mess around until his design is complete. Have him wash and dry his hands thoroughly, then place a large sheet of paper on top of the fingerpainting. Rub all over the back of the paper with clean, dry hands. Slowly lift the paper off the table and hang to dry.

Crayon Melt Prints (#244)

As this activity requires the use of a food warming tray or electric griddle, close supervision by an adult is recommended.

Food warming tray or electric griddle
Aluminum foil
Crayons
Drawing paper
Oven mitts
Damp cloth

Cover the food warming tray with aluminum foil. Set on low setting and when the tray is warm, make a crayon design on the foil. The crayon will melt as you draw and produce beautiful, colourful designs. To make the print, lay paper over the crayon design and carefully smooth the paper down with oven mitts. Lift it off and see the design transferred to the paper. Wipe the foil clean with a damp cloth and start again for a new print.

String Block Printing (#245)

String or rope
Small blocks of wood
Tempera paint in a shallow pan
Paper

Wrap string or rope around a small block of wood several times and tie it in place (make sure the rope is distributed evenly over the block, not wrapped in one spot). Press the string block into the paint then press onto paper. Move the block around in different directions, and add different colours until an interesting design is obtained.

Paper Batik (#246)

> Construction paper
> Crayons
> Tempera paints and brush
> Newspaper
> Drawing paper
> Hot iron

Have your child completely color a piece of construction paper with crayons. Show him how to crumple the paper carefully into a tight ball, then gently unfold the picture and notice how the surface has cracked. Brush contrasting paint over the paper to create a mosaic effect. When the picture has dried, place it on a sheet of newspaper and cover with a piece of thin drawing paper. Using a patting motion, iron over the drawing paper with a hot iron to smooth out the cracks in the original paper and transfer the original image to the drawing paper.

SCULPTING

Sculpting, creating three-dimensional structures, challenges a child's imagination. Not only is it artistic, but gushing around with *Super Goop* and other modelling compounds can also encourage a scientific interest in your child (science begins as a "hands-on" activity).

Many different materials can be used for sculpting. Your child is probably familiar with playdough and modelling clay (see Chapter 2), but here are some different ideas you may want to try.

Super Goop (#247)

> 2 cups water
> 1/2 cup cornstarch
> Food colouring
> Saucepan
> Mixing spoon
> Ziplock bags (optional)

Boil water in saucepan. Add cornstarch and stir until smooth. Add food colouring and stir. Remove from heat and cool. Let your child squish away on the tabletop, or for less mess (or younger children) pour into two ziplock bags and seal. Your child can squish the bag or trace letters, numbers or shapes on the outside of the bag.

Whipped Snow (#248)

2 cups warm water
1 cup pure laundry soap or soap flakes
Electric mixer
Large bowl

Put water and soap in a large bowl and beat with electric mixer until very fluffy. Add colour if desired. This can be molded into shapes and left to dry.

Homemade Silly Putty (#249)

2 parts white glue
1 part liquid starch
Small mixing bowl

Mix well and let dry until it is workable. You may have to add a bit more glue or starch. (This may not work well on a humid day.) Experiment! Store in an airtight container.

Plaster Hand & Footprints (#250)

Patch plaster or plaster of Paris
Water
Tin can
Mixing spoon
Paper plates

To make plaster mix, stir 2 cups of patch plaster or plaster of Paris and 1-1/4 cups water in a tin can. It should be as thick as pea soup so it can cast without air bubbles. Plaster of Paris dries in about 10-20 minutes, while patch plaster takes 20-40 minutes to dry.

To make a cast of your child's hand or footprint, pour 1" of plaster mix into a paper plate. Wait 2 minutes for plaster of Paris, 6 minutes for patch plaster. Have your child press his hand or foot gently into the plaster so it doesn't go right to the bottom. Hold for 1 to 2 minutes and remove. Let the imprint sit overnight, then peel the plate from the print. Glue a picture hook to the back and hang it on your child's wall.

Sugar Cube Sculpture (#251)

Sugar cubes
Glue
Styrofoam meat trays or a piece of heavy cardboard
Food colouring or tempera paint

Let your child create wonderful sculptures by gluing sugar cubes onto a styrofoam meat tray or heavy cardboard and onto each other. You can colour the cubes by quickly dipping them into food colouring, or by lightly dabbing on some tempera paint.

PAPIER MÂCHÉ

Papier mâché can be a very messy activity, but is a lot of fun for children and adults alike. Papier mâché is a special kind of paper modeling that uses paste in combination with paper such as newsprint, paper toweling, gift wrap, crepe paper, tissue paper, construction paper or aluminum foil. Paper can be torn into 2" squares or long strips or larger squares. Torn edges glue better and result in a more interesting finished appearance.

For young children, a basic flour-and-water paste is the best bonding material to use. Begin with 1 cup of water; mix in about 1/4 cup of flour until the mixture is thin and runny. Stir this mixture into 5 cups lightly boiling water. Gently boil and stir for 2 to 3 minutes. Cool until you can dip the paper into it.

Pour the paste into a shallow tray. Dip strips of paper into the tray, or brush paste on with a paint brush. Paste the strips over a form such as an inflated balloon, an empty toilet paper or paper towel roll, or even crumpled newspaper. Add as many layers as you like; model the form with your fingers as you go. Tissue paper can be used as the final layer for a colourful finish.

Papier Mâché Bracelet (#252)

Cardboard tube or baby bottle
Scissors
Papier mâché paste
Newsprint or other paper
Coloured tissue paper or paint

For this project you will need a cardboard tube large enough in diamater to slip over your child's hand. Cut 1" or 2" pieces of the tube and cover with layers of paper and paste. Finish with brightly coloured strips of tissue paper or paint. Or instead of using a cardboard tube form, mold strips of paper around a bottle with the appropriate diameter. Grease or powder the bottle, then start with a layer of newsprint. Add a layer of heavier construction paper for strength, then an additional six layers of papier mâché. Remove the bracelet from the bottle and finish with paint or strips of tissue paper.

Papier Mâché Hat (#253)

Papier mâché paste
Two large squares of wrapping paper
String
Paint

To make a fancy hat shaped to fit each individual head, paste together two big squares of wrapping paper. Set this on your child's head, mold the crown of the hat, and tie string around your child's forehead to hold the shape. After 10 minutes, remove the hat, shape, let dry and paint.

Papier Mâché Piñata (#254)

Large inflated balloon
String
Newsprint or other paper
Papier mâché paste
Small toys and candy
Crepe paper or tissue paper
Paints

This is a great project to make for a birthday party or other special occasion. Hang a big balloon from a string and cover with many layers of paper and paste, leaving a hole about 6" in diameter at the top of the balloon, around the string. This will take several days to dry. When dry, pop the balloon and pour in toys and candy, then cover the opening with more paper and paste. Let dry again, then decorate the outside with fringed crepe paper or paints. Have the children try to break the pinata by taking turns swinging at it with a play baseball bat or golf club.

CUTTING & PASTING

Most young children gain enormous pleasure from the use of scissors and the feel of paste. Buy your child a decent pair of scissors and teach him scissor safety. Show him how to keep the edges sharp by cutting sandpaper.

Paste can be store-bought white glue, or use one of the glue or paste recipes in Chapter 2. Glue and paste is best applied with a small paint brush, although popsicle sticks or plastic applicators from the art store can also be used. For variety, add food colouring to glue before using.

Keep a stack of old magazines and catalogues on hand for cutting. An old wallpaper book is also great for all the interesting shapes it contains. Cut out circles, squares, rectangles, triangles or other creative shapes and glue onto construction paper to make all kinds of designs and pictures.

Funny Face (#255)

    Old magazines
    Scissors
    Paper
    Glue

Look through old magazines, searching for pictures of faces, and cut out as many eyes, noses, mouths, ears and heads of hair as you can find. Mix them up and have your child piece together a funny face, then paste it onto a piece of paper.

Tissue Art (#256)

    Glue
    Paper cup or small plastic container
    Water
    Paint brush
    Paper
    Tissue paper cut into 1/2"x16" strips
    Scissors
    Sequins, beads, glitter (optional)

Pour a small amount of glue into a paper cup or small plastic container and add about 1/4 cup water to make it the consistency of paint. Have your child paint the glue solution onto a piece of paper, then crumple up strips of brightly coloured tissue paper and press them onto the paper. Use a variety of colours and add sequins, beads and glitter for a real piece of art.

Chinese Lantern (#257)

> Construction paper
> Scissors
> Glue or stapler

Fold construction paper in half the long way and show your child how to cut from the folded edge to within 1-1/2" of the opposite side. When cuts have been made along the entire length of the paper, unfold and form into a cylinder by joining the short uncut ends of paper together. Glue or staple on another strip of construction paper for a handle.

Personal Puzzle (#258)

> Old magazines, catalogs or greeting cards
> Photograph of your child (optional)
> Cardboard
> Glue
> Scissors

Using pictures from a magazine or catalog, greeting cards, or an enlarged photograph of your child, make personal puzzles by gluing the picture onto a piece of cardboard which has been cut the same size. When dry, let your child cut the picture into pieces to create his own puzzle. Puzzles are great for helping your child recognize shapes, a prerequisite to learning letters and numbers.

Torn Tissue Design (#259)

> Coloured tissue paper
> White glue
> Paint brush
> White poster board
> Acrylic polymer (optional)
> Synthetic paint brush (optional)

Have your child tear various colours of tissue paper into large pieces. Brush white glue thinned with water onto the back of each piece and arrange them on a piece of white poster board. Show your child how to create new colours by overlapping two different pieces; yellow over red makes orange, light blue over pink makes purple, etc. To give a nice sheen to the finished product, coat it with acrylic polymer using a synthetic paint brush (available at an art supply store).

Picture Placemat (#260)

Family photographs
Cardboard or construction paper
Glue
Clear contact paper

Give your child the family photographs that don't quite make it into your photo album. Have him glue them onto a piece of cardboard or construction paper and cover with clear contact paper to make a placemat. This makes a great gift for Daddy or Grandma.

Circle Bear (#261)

Brown and white construction paper
Scissors
Glue
Black marker or crayon

Cut circles of brown construction paper to make a circle bear. You will need one large circle for the body, two small circles for paws, a medium circle for the head, and two half circles for ears. Show your child how to glue them onto white construction paper to form a bear. Your child can use a black marker to draw a face on the bear. You can also cut out smaller white circles to glue into place on the paws, ears, and tummy.

Gingerbread People (#262)

Thin cardboard or brown construction paper
Pen or marker
Scissors
Glue
Lace, ribbon, fabric scraps
Pieces of cereal, small candy or licorice

Using thin cardboard or brown construction paper, draw the outline of a gingerbread girl or boy. Your child can cut it out and glue on bits of lace and ribbon or scraps of fabric for clothes. Make a face out of cereal or candy.

Shadow Silhouette (#263)

Bright light
Construction paper
Tape
Scissors
Glue

Have your child stand sideways to the wall and shine a bright light on him so that his profile makes a shadow on the wall. Tape a piece of construction paper so that the shadow falls on it and trace around your child's silhouette. Have him cut it out and mount it on another piece of construction paper in a contrasting colour.

Tissue Paper Mirror (#264)

Cardboard
Scissors
Aluminum foil
Glue
Tissue paper cut into 4" squares

Cut cardboard into the shape of a hand mirror. Cut a piece of aluminum foil into a corresponding shape and glue to one side to use as a mirror. Have your child crumple 4" squares of coloured tissue paper into balls for flowers and glue them close together on the other side of the mirror.

Foil Wrapping Paper (#265)

Heavy-duty aluminum foil
Coloured tissue paper
Acrylic polymer
Synthetic paint brush

Make your own foil wrapping paper with heavy duty aluminum foil, tissue paper and acrylic polymer (available at an art supply store). Tear or cut up pieces of tissue paper and arrange on the aluminum foil. Mix the acrylic polymer with a little water and brush all over the foil, letting it soak through. It will make the paper stick to the foil and give it a really glossy finish.

Jelly Bean Picture (#266)

Cardboard
Glue
Jelly beans

Help your child draw a picture with glue on a piece of cardboard. Have him place jelly beans on the glue. You can give this a seasonal theme by using pastel coloured jelly beans on a picture of a rabbit for Easter, or make a Christmas tree with green jelly beans and use beans in other colours for lights and decorations.

Eggshell Mosaic (#267)

Coloured eggshells
Construction paper
Crayon, pen or marker
Glue

This is a great way to use up the remains of the Easter eggs. Your child will have a lot of fun breaking up all the eggshells, and the pretty colours make a great mosaic. On a piece of construction paper, have your child draw a simple design. Fill it in with glue and add the bits of coloured eggshell. If you don't have coloured eggshells available, dye your eggshells just as you would dye hard-boiled eggs (see Chapter 9).

Favourite Foods (#268)

Old magazines
Scissors
Glue
Paper plate
Pipe cleaner
Tape

Have your child cut pictures of his favourite foods from old magazines. Paste them onto a paper plate and hang from the wall by taping a curved pipe cleaner onto the back. Or make a placemat by gluing the pictures onto a piece of construction paper and covering with clear contact paper.

CRAFTS & OTHER FUN THINGS TO MAKE

Not only will craft projects challenge your child's imagination and artistic ability, they will fill in many hours of a rainy afternoon and help keep your child stimulated and happy. Make crafts as gifts for friends and family, or use them to brighten up your child's room and the rest of the house. Most of these projects can be made using objects found around the house or collected on your daily walks.

Playdough Jewellery (#269)

Playdough
Toothpick or large, blunt needle
Clear gloss enamel or nail polish
String

Roll small pieces of playdough into balls for beads. Pierce each bead with a toothpick or large blunt needle and allow to dry for several days. Check holes after a day to see if they need repunching. When dry, coat with clear gloss enamel or clear nail polish to bring out the colour. Thread beads onto a string and knot the ends together to create a necklace or bracelet.

Homemade Fan (#270)

Paper
Crayons or markers

Have your child draw a design on a piece of construction paper or plain paper and show him how to make a fan by folding the paper back and forth in 1" folds.

Spoon People (#271)

Wooden kitchen spoon
Scissors
Glue
Yarn
Buttons
Marker

Use a wooden kitchen spoon to make a spoon person. Have your child glue on yarn for hair and buttons for eyes. Draw on a mouth and nose with markers. Make several of these for a spoon family, and encourage your child to tell a story with these little people.

Framed Flowers   (#272)

Flowers or leaves
Crayon shavings
Wax paper
Newspaper
Iron

Go out on a walk with your child and pick some pretty spring flowers or fall leaves. At home, make shavings of brightly coloured crayons with a grater or knife. Place a piece of wax paper, wax side up, on top of several layers of newspaper on your work surface. Arrange the flowers or leaves and crayon shavings on top of the wax paper, then cover with another piece of wax paper, wax side down. Place several layers of newspaper over top and iron thoroughly until the crayons are melted. Hang to dry. A smaller version glued to one half of a folded piece of construction paper makes a unique and beautiful greeting card.

Coffee Can Cannisters   (#273)

Empty coffee cans
Paintings, drawings or other artwork your child has made
Scissors
Glue
Clear contact paper

Use paintings, drawings or other artwork your child has made to create some decorative and useful cannisters out of empty coffee cans. Cut the artwork to size so that it is as high as the coffee can and wide enough to wrap all the way around with some overlap. Place glue on each vertical edge of the wrong side of the artwork. Evenly space two or three more vertical lines of glue over the wrong side of the paper and press onto the coffee can, overlapping the edges. To protect the artwork, cover with clear contact paper. These cannisters are great for holding crayons, playdough and cookie cutters, or small toy pieces, or try "wrapping" a birthday gift in the decorated can.

Binoculars   (#274)

Two toilet paper rolls
Tape
Markers, crayons, stickers, etc.

Tape two toilet paper rolls together to make a pair of binoculars for your child. He can decorate them with markers, stickers, etc., and use them to spot interesting things as you go for a walk or ride in the car.

Wax Paper Art (#275)

Newspaper
Wax paper
Crayons
Grater or knife
Hot iron

Place several layers of newspaper on your work surface. Place wax paper on top of newspaper, wax side up. Shave, chop finely or grate crayons onto the wax paper. Place a second sheet of wax paper, wax side down, on top of the first (so that crayon pieces are between). Cover with several layers of newspaper and iron until crayons are melted. Hang to dry.

Waxed Leaves (#276)

Leaves
Newspaper
Wax paper
Iron

On a fall walk with your child, collect several different types and colors of leaves. At home, cover your ironing board with several layers of newspaper, then place a sheet of wax paper on top. Have your child arrange his leaves on top of the wax paper. Place a second sheet of wax paper over the leaves. Cover with a layer of newspaper and place a medium hot iron on top. Hold the iron in place for about 30 seconds and continue until all areas of the wax paper have been heated. Lift off the paper and remove the leaves. They should be waxed enough to retain their shape. Arrange them in a vase or use them in some other art work.

Rainbow Fan (#277)

Paint sample cards
Hole puncher
Paper fastener
Yarn or string

Pick up some colourful paint sample cards from your local hardware store and make a striped rainbow fan. Punch holes in the center of each end of the cards. At one end, join the cards with a paper fastener. At the other, lace yarn through the holes in each card to form the top of the fan.

Pasta Picture (#278)

Pasta in various shapes
Paper plate or piece of cardboard
Glue
Tempera paint

Glue various shapes of pasta onto a paper plate or a piece of cardboard and paint with tempera paints. A variation on this: dye the pasta ahead of time by mixing 1/2 cup of alcohol with food colouring. The larger the pasta the longer it will take to absorb the colour. Dry the pasta on newspaper covered with wax paper, then use to create a pasta picture.

Party Hats (#279)

Construction paper
Crayons, markers, stickers for decorating
Tape or stapler
Scissors
Elastic thread or ribbon

Let your child decorate a piece of construction paper with crayons, markers, stickers, etc. Make a party hat by folding the paper into a cone shape, tape or staple together, and cut the bottom edge so that it is even. Staple a length of elastic thread or ribbon to each side to hold the hat on.

Paper Bag Kite (#280)

Large paper bag
Hole puncher
Paper ring reinforcements
Scissors
String
Paint or markers
Stapler or glue
Crepe paper streamers

Punch a hole on each of the four corners of a large paper bag, at least 1" from the edge of the bag. Place a paper ring reinforcement on each hole. Cut two 3 ft. lengths of string and tie each end into a hole to form two loops. Cut another 3 ft. length of string and tie it through the two loops to act as a handle. Decorate the bag with paint or markers and glue or staple on crepe paper streamers. When your child holds onto the string and runs, the kite will fill with air and float behind him.

Pinwheel (#281)

Plain or construction paper
Crayons, markers, glitter or stickers for decorating
Scissors
Paper fastener
Cardboard cut into a small circle
Straw, wooden dowel or unsharpened pencil

Have your child decorate a square piece of paper with crayons, markers, paint, stickers, glitter, etc. Mark the center of the square and cut from each corner into the center within one inch. Fold every other point into the center and tape, making sure the decorated side of the paper is on the outside. Push a paper fastener through a small circular piece of cardboard, then through the center of the pinwheel. Fasten around a straw, wooden dowel or unsharpened pencil.

Noodle Necklace (#282)

Macaroni noodles
String
Tempera paint
Brush

Make a noodle necklace by threading macaroni noodles on a string. Knot the ends together and paint with tempera paints. Let dry before wearing your creation.

Egg Carton Butterfly (#283)

Cardboard egg carton
Tempera paint and brush
Pipe cleaners
Construction paper
Scissors
Stapler

Cut the egg carton in half lengthwise. Turn one of the halves upside down and paint with tempera paint. Attach pipe cleaners to the head for feelers. Cut wings from construction paper and decorate with paint or markers; staple to the side of the carton. Use your imagination to make variations of the egg carton butterfly; use one cup of the carton to make turtles or ladybugs; use three cups to make little bumblebees; use a full half carton to make a caterpillar.

Modern Art (#284)

Piece of cardboard or paper plate
Glue or paste
Small household items (cereal, buttons, macaroni, sequins, etc.)

Give your child a strong piece of cardboard or a paper plate, some glue, and small items of different sizes, shapes and textures, eg. cereal, buttons, macaroni, sequins, cut up straws, plastic juice jug lids, etc. He can be as creative as he wants to be with his own version of modern art.

Paper Doll Chain (#285)

Large sheets of paper or newspaper
Scissors
Crayons or markers

Make a chain of paper dolls for your child by folding a large sheet of paper like a fan (newspaper, a cut-open paper bag or computer paper works well). The fan folds should be as wide as you want your dolls to be. Draw your doll shape with arms and legs held away from the body, so that the hands and feet fall on the folds. Cut out the shape of the doll, taking care not to cut the folds at the hands and feet, or you will end up with a lot of single paper dolls instead of a chain. Unfold the chain and let your child decorate each doll with crayons or markers. With a little practice, your child will soon be able to make a doll chain on his own.

Paper Bag Vest (#286)

Large brown paper bag
Scissors
Paint

Make a vest from brown paper bags by cutting a head hole, arm holes, and a fringe along the bottom. Your child can paint it and when dry, try it on.

Napkin Rings (#287)

Empty paper towel or toilet paper rolls
Scissors
Crayons, paints, stickers or glitter

Make napkin rings for a special occasion or to give as a gift.Cut empty paper towel or toilet paper rolls into 1-1/2" pieces. Have your child decorate them with crayons, paints, stickers or glitter.

Picture Frame (#288)

Jar lid
Photograph
Pen
Scissors
Glue
Magnets
Ribbon

Place a jar lid (baby food jar lids work well) on the photograph you wish to frame and trace around it. Cut out the photo and glue it inside the lid. If you like, tie a ribbon around the outside of the lid. Glue a magnet onto the back of the lid and place it on the refrigerator.

Feather Headband (#289)

Construction paper
Scissors
Stapler
Glue

Make a feather headband for your child by cutting a strip of brown construction paper about 1-1/2" wide. Measure the length by placing the headband around his head and stapling the ends together to fit snugly. Cut several feather shapes out of coloured construction paper, or gather some real feathers on a walk, and glue to the headband. Your child can draw a design on the headband with markers or crayons if he wishes.

Picture Soap (#290)

Bar of soap
Glue
Photograph or other picture
Paint brush
Wax
Small empty can
Hot water

Glue a photograph or picture cut out of a magazine onto a bar of soap. Melt wax in a small empty can in a pan of hot water. To waterproof, dip a paint brush in melted wax and paint it over the picture. Your child can take a bath with his special soap, or save it to give as a gift.

Egg Carton Flowers (#291)

Empty egg cartons
Scissors
Paint, markers or crayons
Pipe cleaner
Green construction paper
Glue

Cut apart an egg carton into individual sections and have your child paint each section in a variety of colours. (Markers or crayons can also be used.) Poke a pipe cleaner through the bottom of each section to make a stem. Cut leaf shapes out of green construction paper and glue onto the pipe cleaner. Several flowers of different colours in a bud vase makes a great gift or table centrepiece.

Toy Boats (#292)

Styrofoam meat trays
Straw
Paper
Scissors
Tape

Make toy sailboats with clean styrofoam meat trays. Insert a straw into the tray for the mast. Cut triangular sails from white construction paper and tape to the straw. Your child can sail his boat in the bathtub, swimming pool or a tub of water.

Straw Holders (#293)

Thin cardboard
Scissors
Hole puncher
Crayons, markers, stickers for decorating
Straws

This is a great project for a special occasion or holiday, or just to make any day special. Using thin cardboard (a paper plate or file folder works well), cut out a square, circle or special shape (like a heart for Valentine's Day). Use a hole puncher to make a hole at the top and bottom of your cutout, then have your child decorate with crayons, markers or stickers. Insert a drinking straw into one hole and out the other. Your child can then use this to drink his favourite beverage. This is a good idea for placecards for a birthday or other occasion.

Parade Shaker (#294)

Paper towel roll
Stapler
Crepe paper
Scissors

Decorate an empty paper towel roll by stapling several 12" strips of crepe paper to each end of the roll. Cut each strip into thirds and scrunch it with your fingers to make the shaker look fuller. Let your little one have his own parade by holding onto the roll and shaking the streamer.

Bird Feeder (#295)

Pine cone
Peanut butter
Knife
Bird seed
String

Make your own bird feeder with peanut butter, a pine cone and bird seed. Thoroughly cover the pine cone with peanut butter, then roll it in bird seed. Hang it outside near a window and your child can watch the birds eat.

Rock Art (#296)

Rocks
Glue
Paint
Playdough or fabric scraps

Make rock people or rock animals by gluing together rocks you have collected on a walk. Your child can then paint his rock art, and add accessories made out of playdough or scraps of fabric, ribbon or lace.

Cookie Cutter Cards (#297)

Construction paper
Crayon, pen or marker
Scraps of fabric or lace, paper doilies, glitter, stickers, etc.

Fold a piece of plain or construction paper in half to make a greeting card. Have your child trace around cookie cutters in appropriate shapes, eg. hearts for Valentines, trees or angels for Christmas. The card can then be decorated with scraps of fabric or lace, paper doilies, glitter, stickers, etc.

Styrofoam People (#298)

Styrofoam balls and blocks in different sizes
Toothpicks
Scraps of yarn and fabric
Glue
Markers or paint

Use toothpicks to join the styrofoam shapes together to form people, a snowman, animals, etc. Glue on scraps of yarn and fabric for hair and clothes. Use markers or paint to add faces or other details.

Coat Rack (#299)

Four eight-penny nails
One-foot length of 1"x2" wood
Hammer
Paint, markers or crayons

This is something your child can make that is useful, and a good gift for someone special. Show your child how to hammer four eight-penny nails into a one-foot length of 1"x2" wood. The wood can then be painted with tempera paints, markers or crayons. Be sure to display this in a prominent place.

Tall Trees (#300)

Newspaper
Tape
Scissors
Empty toilet paper or paper towel roll
Piece of heavy cardboard

Roll up the long side of one sheet of newspaper and tape it closed. Cut one end of the roll into a fringe using long snips, fairly close together. Reaching inside the fringed end of the roll, carefully pull out the centre to make the tree spiral up until it's tall. The fringes become the leaves of the tree; curl them or dress them up with paper flowers. To display your tree, stand it in an empty toilet paper or paper towel roll taped to a cardboard base.

9.

Holiday Activities

*"The first holiday may have been invented to celebrate
fertility or planting or harvest, but we're sure a mother was
behind it. Even then she must have known that nothing could
cure her day-to-day drudgery as well as a holiday or
brighten the eye of a small child so quickly."*

Marguerite Kelly and Elia Parsons

Nothing can disrupt your daily routine like a holiday, yet nothing is quite so
important. Mothers and small children alike often need the lift of a special
day on which we can focus our energy and attention. In addition to
celebrating birthdays and traditional holidays, make the most of each small
victory and accomplishment. You don't have to go all out all the time; putting
a candle on the dinner table and using your best china can make even an
ordinary day extraordinary. Most of the fun and excitement comes from the
anticipation that builds as the celebration draws near, so be sure to allow your
child to take part in the planning and preparation for each festivity.

BIRTHDAY CELEBRATIONS

For the first few years of your child's life, a family dinner complete with
birthday cake and candles is probably all that is required in the way of a

birthday celebration. But somewhere around the third or fourth year, your child will probably want to start inviting a few friends over for a "real" birthday party. This will usually be about two hours long, and consist mainly of eating and opening gifts. Keep the food simple; sandwiches, pizza, hotdogs, carrot sticks, fruit, juice, and chocolate milk are some suggestions. Older children will enjoy a few simple games such as London Bridge, Pin the Tail on the Donkey, *Follow the Leader, Red Light/Green Light,* or *Simon Says*. If you really want to go all out and organize a theme party for your child, there are many excellent birthday party books available in bookstores or at your local library.

If you find the commercialism of even a small child's party appalling, you may want to consider asking each mother to spend not more than a few dollars on a present. You can also be good to the environment and avoid spending a small fortune on matching hats, plates, cups, napkins and tablecloth by using brightly coloured linen and unbreakable plates. Have each child make her own party hat with construction paper, markers, stickers and glitter (see *Party Hat*s on page 115) and substitute a small, wrapped gift for each child in place of a "goodie bag". Always send thank-you notes for gifts received using your child's original artwork in place of store-bought cards.

Birthday Time Capsule (#301)

> Envelope
> Writing paper
> Pen

This is a wonderful tradition for young and old alike. Each person on their birthday prepares certain information to be put into their "time capsule". For young children ask questions and write down their responses. You may want to ask questions about favourite foods, songs, activities, friends, etc. Ask what your child is looking forward to over the year, and what she expects life to be like next year on her birthday. When everything is written down, place the paper in an envelope and mark the birthday person's name on it and the *Date to be Opened* (next year on her birthday). You'll all have a lot of fun when the time capsule is opened.

Video Time Capsule (#302)

> Video camera
> Video tape

If you have access to a video camera, consider taping your *Birthday Time Capsule* instead of writing it down. You will need to ask questions of a younger child, while older children may enjoy just talking about themselves and their day-to-day life. Once the time capsule is taped, put the tape away and don't watch it until the following year on your child's birthday. If doing this for more than one child, use a different tape for each, but use the tape only for the time capsule. Over the years you will be able to watch your child grow up on her time capsule tape.

Super Chocolate Birthday Cake (#303)

This chocolate cake is quick and easy to make, and is absolutely delicious. After the cake is baked and cooled, insert foil-wrapped coins into one of the layers before frosting. When cutting the cake, be sure each child receives a piece with a coin in it. You may not want to include coins in a cake for very young children because of the danger of choking.

    2 cups white sugar
    6 Tbsp. butter
    2 eggs
    1 cup cocoa (fill with boiling water to make two cups of liquid)
    2 cups flour
    2 tsp. baking powder
    1 tsp. soda
    1 cup boiling water

Cream sugar and butter; add beaten egg and cocoa liquid. Mix soda and boiling water. Add this and remaining ingredients, mix well, and pour into two greased 8" or 9" layer cake pans. Bake for 30 minutes at 350o.

Fudgy Chocolate Frosting

    3 Tbsp. melted butter
    1/4 cup cocoa
    1/4 cup milk
    1/2 tsp. vanilla
    2 cups sifted icing sugar

Combine melted butter with cocoa. Blend in milk, vanilla and sifted icing sugar until smooth. Frosts one two-layer 8" or 9" cake.

NEW YEAR'S DAY

The beginning of a new year is a time for a fresh start, a time for new beginnings. Whether you celebrate with a traditional family dinner or eat take-out Chinese food, the arrival of a new year is indeed an occasion worth celebrating.

New Year's Day is often the time we assess ourselves and set goals for our future. By adapting the *Birthday Time Capsule* or *Video Time Capsule* ideas on page 124 you can begin a New Year's tradition for your family that you and your child will cherish for years to come.

Friends Far & Near (#304)

Christmas cards you have received
Basket

After Christmas is over, place the cards you have received into a basket and set it on your table. Starting in January, take one card out of the basket each day and talk about that person or family with your child. If prayers are a part of your child's bedtime routine, this is a good way to include someone special each night.

VALENTINE'S DAY

Valentine's Day is the day for celebrating love. Start your preparations several weeks in advance as you make heart-shaped cookies, cards, and Valentine crafts. On February 14th, dress the whole family in red and put your heart-shaped cookie cutter to work for toast, sandwiches, apples, cheese and *Finger Jello* (see Chapter 4). A small Valentine's party can be a simple and fun way to celebrate this special day.

Heart People (#305)

Construction paper in red, white and pink
Glue or paste

Using red, white and pink construction paper, trace and cut different sizes of hearts ranging in size from two to six inches. Glue the hearts together in different combinations to form heart people, using large hearts for head and body, smaller ones for arms, legs, etc. You can also try making heart animals.

Valentine Chain (#306)

Construction paper in red, white and pink
Glue or paste

Cut strips of red, white and pink construction paper, three to four inches long and one-half to one inch wide. Form a circle with one strip, gluing the ends together. Take the next strip and loop it through the first circle, again gluing the ends together. Continue on and make a chain as long as you want. Use to decorate doorways, walls, etc.

Valentine Placemat (#307)

Valentines your child has received
Construction paper or light cardboard
Glue or paste
Clear contact paper

Have your child glue her favourite valentines onto a large piece of construction paper or cardboard. Cover this collage with clear contact paper to make a placemat.

Heart Window Decorating (#308)

Plain or construction paper
Scissors
Can of spray-on artificial snow

Fold several pieces of paper in half and cut out heart shapes in varying sizes. Use the pieces of paper that the hearts have been cut out of as stencils. Tape them to the window in an interesting arrangement and spray with artifical snow. Remove the stencils to see the heart shapes on the window.

Valentine Mobile (#309)

Valentines your child has received
Thread or yarn
Hole puncher
Thread or yarn

Have your child punch holes in her valentines, thread and hang from a hanger to create a mobile. Hang the finished mobile from a curtain rod.

Heart Necklace   (#310)

Plain or construction paper
Scissors
Liquid tempera paint
Hole punch
Yarn
Photo of your child (optional)
Glue (optional)

Out of plain or construction paper, cut a heart shape big enough for your child's hand to fit on. Dip her hand in liquid tempera paint and press it on the paper. When it is dry, punch a hole in the top and string yarn through to make a necklace. Write a Valentine's message on it, and glue a picture of your child on the other side if you wish. Send or give it to a special friend or relative.

Valentine Cookies   (#311)

Rolled cookie dough
Heart-shaped cookie cutters
Pink icing
Sprinkles or other candy to decorate with

Make up a batch of *Cookie Cut-outs* (Chapter 4) or use another rolled cookie dough recipe. Cut out heart shapes in various sizes and bake as directed. Ice with pink icing and decorate with sprinkles or other candy.

EASTER

Easter is the traditional Christian holiday celebrating the resurrection of Jesus Christ. It is also a time to celebrate the coming of spring and all the joyous signs of new life that abound. Consider holding a small Easter party for your child and a few friends. Make some *Easter Bunny Ears* and decorate eggs with your guests. Have an informal Easter parade with decorated wagons and tricycles. An Easter egg or candy hunt can be held either indoors or out, depending on the weather. Remember that for children the fun is in the planning and anticipation, so start your Easter crafts and activities early.

Easter Grass (#312)

Large Easter basket
Wheat seeds (about 1 lb.)
Vermiculite (about 1 lb.)
Plastic wrap

Grow a miniature meadow right in your own Easter basket. About a week before Easter, line a large Easter basket with plastic wrap and fill with vermiculite to 2" below the rim. Sprinkle the wheat seeds on top of the vermiculite, set the basket in the sink and add water until the seed bed is moist. You won't have to water it again before Easter. Set the basket in a pan and place in filtered sunlight. Cover loosely with plastic wrap to keep moist; remove the plastic after two days. The wheat will begin to sprout during the next few days, and by Easter morning you will have real Easter grass to hide your eggs in.

Easter Bunny Mask (#313)

Paper plate
Pink construction paper
Pink or white pipe cleaners
Yarn

Using a paper plate, cut out the eyes and nose. Cut out bunny ears from pink construction paper and glue to the plate. Use pipe cleaners for whiskers, and attach two pieces of yarn on either side of the plate to tie onto your little bunny's head.

Paper Plate Easter Bunny (#314)

Large paper plate
Small paper plate
Glue
Pink construction paper
Cotton ball
Crayons or markers

Using a small and large paper plate, glue the smaller plate to the large one to form the head and body of the bunny. Cut out bunny ears from pink construction paper and glue or staple to the head. Draw on the bunny face with crayons or markers, and glue a cotton ball on the back for the tail.

Easter Bunny Ears (#315)

Construction paper in white and pink
Glue

Using white and pink construction paper, cut out bunny ear shapes, two white and two pink, the pink being slightly smaller. Glue the pink ears onto the white ears. Glue the ears onto a long strip of construction paper, measure and staple to form a headband for your child.

Papier Mâché Easter Egg (#316)

For additional information on papier mâché, see Chapter 8.

Papier mâché paste
Balloon
Tape
1" torn strips of newspaper or paper towel
Pie tin
Paint
Paint brushes
Coloured tissue paper (optional)
Shellac

Mix up some papier mâché paste (see Chapter 2) and put it in a pie tin. Blow up the balloon and tape it to the top of the table. Dip strips of newspaper in the paste and place them on the balloon, overlapping edges slightly. Cover the balloon completely and let dry. You can decorate the covered balloon by painting on an Easter egg design, or cover with an additional layer of tissue paper in pastel Easter colours. Finish with shellac for a shiny, glazed effect.

EGG DECORATING

There are many different ways to decorate an Easter egg without using commercially prepared egg dyes. If you do want to dye eggs you can make your own dye with food colouring or vegetables. But you can also make pretty eggs using crayons, paint, fabric, yarn, seeds ... many different materials to create many different effects. Once you get going you'll come up with your own ideas as you start to experiment. Here are just a few to get you started.

If you are using hard-boiled eggs they should be kept refrigerated. Do not eat them if they are not refrigerated or have been sprayed with acrylic. If you are creating a special work of art, you should use blown eggs instead of hard-boiled. They are more fragile, and probably not a good idea for really young children, but you can keep them from year to year.

To blow an egg, poke a small hole at each end of the egg with a large needle. Push the needle inside the egg and twist around until the yoke is broken. Hold the egg over a bowl and blow hard through the hole at the top until the shell is empty. Rinse the eggshells well and allow to dry completely before decorating. (Save the raw eggs and scramble them up for breakfast, or do some baking together.)

Natural Egg Dye (#317)

Hard-boiled or blown eggs
Various food and plant items
Sauce pans (one for each colour)
Slotted spoon
Strainer
Cooking oil and soft cloth

Pour 1/2 cup water into each saucepan and add cut-up fruit, vegetable or plant parts (try carrots, blueberries, grass, coffee...). Bring to a boil and simmer until the water turns the colour you want. Remove from heat and strain, reserving the water. When the water has cooled, add eggs and allow to sit in the water until they turn the desired colour. Remove with a slotted spoon and allow to air dry. Polish dry eggs with a small amount of cooking oil and a soft cloth.

Crepe Paper Egg Dye (#318)

Hard-boiled or blown eggs
Crepe paper (different colours)
Hot water
Small bowls or cups
Slotted spoon
Cooking oil and soft cloth

Soak crepe paper in hot water in a small bowl or cup. Add eggs and allow to sit in the water until they turn the desired colour. Remove with a slotted spoon and allow to air dry. Polish dry eggs with a small amount of cooking oil and a soft cloth.

Food Colouring Egg Dye (#319)

Hard-boiled or blown eggs
Food colouring
Hot water
White vinegar
Small bowls or cups
Slotted spoon
Cooking oil and soft cloth

For each colour desired, measure 1/4 tsp. food colouring into a small bowl or cup. Add 3/4 cup hot water and 1 Tbsp. white vinegar to each colour. Add eggs and allow to sit in the water until they turn the desired colour. Remove with a slotted spoon and allow to air dry. Polish dry eggs with a small amount of cooking oil and a soft cloth.

Marble Eggs (#320)

Hard-boiled or blown eggs
Large glass jar
Hot water
Crayon stubs
Vegetable grater
Waxed paper or newspaper
Empty egg carton
Clear acrylic spray (optional)

Grate peeled crayon stubs over waxed paper or newspaper. Fill the jar with very hot water. Drop pinches of grated crayon into the water and add egg as soon as the crayon begins to melt. Twirl the egg in the water with a spoon; the wax will make a design on the egg. Carefully remove the egg from the water and set it in an upside-down egg carton to dry. Spray with clear acrylic when the wax is dry, if desired.

Sponge Painted Eggs (#321)

Blown or hard-boiled eggs
Liquid tempera paint
Paper cups (one for each paint colour)
Small pieces of sponge or foam
Spring-type clothespins (one for each paint colour)
Egg cups
Clear acrylic spray (optional)

Working on a covered surface, place an egg in an egg cup. Partially fill paper cups with paint. Clip a piece of sponge to a clothespin and dip into the paper cup, using the clothespin as a handle. Lightly dab the sponge over the top half of the egg and let dry. Turn the egg over and repeat. Let the egg dry completely. If you are using blown eggs, spray with clear acrylic for a permanent finish.

Dip & Dye Eggs (#322)

> Hard-boiled eggs
> Masking tape
> Egg dyes in different colours
> Slotted spoon
> Cooking oil and soft cloth

Stick a pattern of masking tape on a plain egg. Dip it in a natural or commercial egg dye and leave it until it is the desired colour. Remove with a slotted spoon and allow to air dry. Remove the masking tape when the egg is completely dry. Leave the masked areas white, or dip the egg again in a lighter dye. Polish the finished eggs with a small amount of cooking oil and a soft cloth.

Waxed Eggs (#323)

> Hard-boiled eggs
> Wax crayons
> Paper towel
> Egg dyes in different colours
> Slotted spoon
> Cooking oil and soft cloth

Draw a heavy crayon pattern on egg and dip it in a natural or commercial egg dye in a dark colour. Leave it in until it is the desired colour. Remove with a slotted spoon and place in a 200° oven for a few minutes to melt the crayon. Wipe with a paper towel and dip again in a lighter colour to fill in the pattern drawn with the crayon. Polish the finished eggs with a small amount of cooking oil and a soft cloth.

THANKSGIVING DAY

While it is traditional to celebrate the harvest with a huge meal of roast turkey and all the trimmings, this year try to emphasize the "giving" in Thanksgiving. Talk with your child about all that you have to be thankful for. This is an ideal time to share your wealth with others and to encourage a giving spirit in your child. Some giving activities you can consider are: collect food in your neighbourhood and take it to the local food bank; do some special baking and take it to a nursing home or to someone who is housebound; take some good usable clothing and toys to a local relief agency; invite someone who is alone to share your Thanksgiving Day celebration.

Thanksgiving Tree (#324)

Construction paper in fall colours
Poster board or cardboard
Scissors
Markers
Glue or paste
Old catalogues or magazines (optional)

Cut leaf shapes out of coloured construction paper. You can draw the shapes on paper and have your child cut them out, or make a leaf pattern your child can trace around herself. Draw a tree trunk and branches on the cardboard or poster board. Ask your child to name things she is thankful for and write them on each leaf (or use pictures cut from old magazines or catalogues). Have your child glue them on the branches. Display in a prominent place as a reminder of your many blessings.

Paper Plate Turkey (#325)

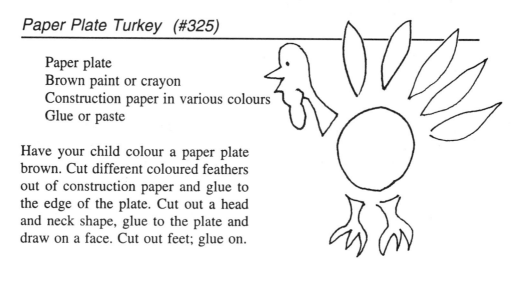

Paper plate
Brown paint or crayon
Construction paper in various colours
Glue or paste

Have your child colour a paper plate brown. Cut different coloured feathers out of construction paper and glue to the edge of the plate. Cut out a head and neck shape, glue to the plate and draw on a face. Cut out feet; glue on.

Thanksgiving Can (#326)

Empty coffee can
Index cards or small pieces of paper
Old magazines
Glue or paste

Several weeks before Thanksgiving, ask your child to tell you what she is thankful for. On index cards or strips of paper, write down the things you talk about. Or have your child search through old magazines for appropriate pictures she can cut out and glue onto index cards. Place the cards inside an empty coffee can. At bedtime, breakfast, or quiet time, have your child reach into the can and remove one card, then talk about what is on the card and why she is thankful for it.

Thanksgiving Placecards (#327)

Yellow construction paper
Brown liquid tempera paint
Pen or marker

Fold a piece of yellow construction paper in half. Dip your child's palm into brown poster paint and carefully print it on the paper. When the paint has dried, make the print look like a turkey; use a pen or marker to add legs, an eye, beak and wattle (the folds of loose red flesh under a turkey's throat). Print the name next to the turkey and use it on the Thanksgiving dinner table as a placecard.

Thanksgiving Placemat (#328)

Old magazines
Construction paper or light cardboard
Glue or paste
Clear contact paper

Give your child old magazines and have her cut out things for which she is thankful. Let her glue them onto a piece of cardboard or construction paper and cover with clear contact paper for a Thanksgiving placemat.

HALLOWEEN

While many people do not celebrate Halloween with its traditional ghoulish emphasis, you can still use it as an excuse for a good costume party. Our children dress in fun, non-scary costumes, and we carve a pumpkin with a big, happy face. Our church throws a wildly successful fall carnival where we eat, play games, and come home with enough candy to last six months.

Regardless of how you celebrate this occasion, here are some fun activities for you and your child to try.

Pom Pom Spider (#329)

Black yarn
Small square of cardboard
Black pipe cleaners
Googly eyes (optional)
Red construction paper (optional)
Glue (optional)

Wind black yarn around and around a square of cardboard until the cardboard is very heavily covered. Using a small piece of yarn, tie securely at the centre, cut edges and remove the cardboard. Insert three pipe cleaners into the knotted center, and bend to form legs. You may need to trim the yarn to form a nice even ball. Glue on googly eyes if desired, or cut eyes out of red construction paper and glue on. Use thread or yarn to hang your spider from the doorway or in the window.

Egg Carton Spider (#330)

Cardboard egg carton
Black pipe cleaners
Black tempera paint, marker or crayon
Red construction paper
Glue
Thread or yarn

Using paint, marker or crayon, colour the cup sections of the egg carton. Cut each egg cup apart; if using paint, wait until the paint has dried. Push pipe cleaner legs into the egg cup and bend so they look like spider's legs. Cut red eyes from the construction paper and glue them on. Use thread or yarn to hang your spiders from the doorway or in the window.

Halloween Chain (#331)

Construction paper in black and orange
Glue or paste

Here's a variation on the traditional Christmas tree decoration. Cut strips of orange and black construction paper, three to four inches long and one-half to one inch wide. Form a circle with one strip, gluing the ends together. Take the next strip and loop it through the first circle, again gluing the ends together. Continue on and make a chain as long as you want. Use to decorate doorways, walls, windows, etc.

Ghost Puppet (#332)

Tissue paper
Cotton ball
Rubber band
String (optional)

Place tissue paper over a cotton ball and secure under the cotton ball with a rubber band. Draw eyes on with a marker. Tie a string around the neck and take it outside to fly, or use it as a finger puppet by hooking it over a finger with a rubber band.

Baked Pumpkin Seeds (#333)

Pumpkin seeds
Cookie sheet
Salt

As you prepare your Thanksgiving or Halloween pumpkin, save the seeds and dry them out. Spread dried seeds on a cookie sheet, salt and quickly broil until lightly browned. Have your child count them into groups of two, three, four, etc., before eating them.

CHRISTMAS

Christmas ... a time for peace on earth and goodwill to all men. A time when Christians the world over traditionally and joyfully celebrate the birth of the baby Jesus. But to our children, is Christmas really a time of peace and joy? We are easily caught up in the excitement of the season: the entertaining and partying, the cooking and baking, the shopping and wrapping. We are physically and emotionally, and sometimes financially, stretched to our limits. A four-year-old may wonder why such a special holiday means only that you no longer have time to read a book or go for a leisurely walk together.

At this busy time of year, we must remember to concentrate on what is important. We must relax and make time for our children and their small and simple pleasures. Go build a snowman, or read a story by the fire. Bake cookies together, or turn out the lights and watch the Christmas tree. Bundle up the family for a tour of your neighbourhood's Christmas lights, then come home to a mug of steaming cocoa. Together you are making Christmas memories that will last a lifetime.

Activity Advent Calendar (#334)

Calendar or weekly planner

In the Christian tradition, Advent begins four Sundays before Christmas, but for this idea the beginning of December is also appropriate. Take out your weekly planner, or bring down your wall calendar and mark down something special to do with your child each day. Stamp and mail your holiday greetings, make some gift wrap together, bake and decorate Christmas cookies, or read a Christmas story by the fire. You can work a lot of your "to do" list into these activities, and planning something special for each day gives you one more way to count down the days to Christmas.

Dip & Dye Snowflakes (#335)

Cone or square-shaped coffee filters or paper towels cut
in a circle or square
Small bowls of dye (diluted food colouring or strong
tempera paint)
Scissors

Fold coffee filters or paper towel in half, quarters, thirds, or any way you want. Dip into a bowl of dye, blot, open up and let dry. When dry, fold again and cut out snowflake lace by cutting small shapes along the folded edges. Use as a holiday decoration; tape to your window or your child's bedroom door.

Jingle Bells (#336)

Bells
Ribbon

Show your child how to string several bells onto a piece of ribbon to make necklaces or bracelets, or string onto your child's shoelaces. Sing "Jingle Bells" as your child jingles through the house.

Snowflake Window Decorating (#337)

Square of plain or construction paper
Scissors
Can of spray-on artificial snow

Fold a square piece of paper into quarters, then fold into a triangle shape. Cut small shapes along the folded edges, then unfold and tape to a window. Spray over the snowflake with artifical snow, and remove to see the design on the window.

Graham Wafer House (#338)

This "gingerbread" house is made with graham wafers and is easier for little hands than one made with traditional gingerbread.

Graham wafers
Cardboard milk carton
Ornamental Frosting (see Chapter 2)
Candy for decorating

Make the icing that holds the house together by following the instructions for *Ornamental Frosting* in Chapter 2. Use the icing to cement graham wafers to the sides of a cardboard milk carton (remember to cover the icing with a damp cloth when you're not using it). Allow the icing to set partially before adding the roof. Decorate with gumdrops, candies, raisins, chocolate chips, Lifesavers, cereal, etc.

Christmas Dough Ornaments (#339)

Make up a batch of dough ornaments (see *Baker's Clay* or *No-Bake Cookie Clay* recipes in Chapter 2). Glue magnets to the backs for Christmas refrigerator decorations, hang from your Christmas tree as ornaments, give as Christmas gifts, or use as a finishing touch on gifts you have wrapped.

Christmas Placemats (#340)

Used greeting cards
Construction paper or light cardboard
Glue or paste
Clear contact paper

Cut up old greetings cards, glue onto a piece of construction paper or light cardboard and cover with clear contact paper for great Christmas placemats.

Homemade Gift Wrap (#341)

Brown paper bags, butcher paper or large sheets of plain paper
Rubber stamps
Ink pads

This is a good activity for Christmas or any time of the year. Not only is it environmentally sound, but homemade gift wrap is far more economical and personal than the commercially-bought wrap, and your child will love to make it, too. Cut open brown paper bags or use butcher paper or large sheets of other plain paper. Using rubber stamps and ink pads in a variety of colors, your child can decorate the paper according to her personal taste. The colors and rubber stamps can be varied according to the season or occasion.

Paper Snowflakes (#342)

White tissue paper cut into squares
Scissors

Fold a square piece of white tissue paper into quarters, then fold into a triangle shape. Cut small shapes along the folded edges, then unfold to see the snowflake. Tape to your window, or around the house for some holiday decorating.

Christmas Countdown (#343)

25 small candy canes, individual pieces of candy, or candy
  kisses (for each child)
One bowl, candy dish or empty coffee can (for each child)

Place 25 small candy canes, kisses or other special candy treats into a bowl, candy dish or empty coffee can. Beginning December 1st, let your child have one treat from her bowl every day. When she begins to ask "How many days 'til Christmas?" (and she will!) she can see for herself by counting the number of candies left in her bowl.

Photo Ornaments (#344)

Photograph of your child
Construction paper
Tape
Glue
Hole punch
Yarn

Draw the shape of a star on construction paper, or cut one out of cardboard and let your child trace it onto the paper, then cut it out. You will need two stars for each ornament. Cut an opening in the middle of one paper star and place your child's photo so that her face looks out the opening. Trim the photo to fit, and tape the edges to the back of the star. Dab glue onto the back edges of the star, and press the second paper star onto it. Punch a hole at the top and thread yarn through; tie to form a hanger for your ornament. Write your child's name and age on the back; she will be proud to hang it on the tree, year after year.

Cinnamon & Applesauce Ornaments (#345)

6 Tbsp. applesauce
10 Tbsp. cinnamon
Cookie cutters
Cookie sheet
Rolling pin
White puff paint (optional)

Mix ingredients together to form dough. Sprinkle additional cinnamon on a bread board or counter and roll out dough 1/4" thick. Cut into shapes and make a hole in the top of each shape so that it can be hung as an ornament. Place on cookie sheet and bake for six hours at 150º with the oven door open. Decorate with white puff paint if desired.

Christmas Giving (#346)

Small toy or gift
Wrapping paper
Tape

Help your child understand the true meaning of Christmas giving. Take her with you to buy a toy or gift for a local charity. Help her wrap it, deliver it together, then stop for a muffin or hot chocolate on your way home.

Christmas Cloves (#347)

Cloves
Oranges

Show your child how to put cloves into an orange for a decoration. Cover the entire orange with cloves and enjoy the Christmas scent.

Glitter Balls (#348)

Styrofoam balls in various sizes
Glue
Glitter in a small shallow dish

Spread glue evenly over a styrofoam ball, then roll in glitter. Allow to dry, then attach a thread for hanging on the Christmas tree.

Holiday Cookies (#349)

Rolled cookie dough
Christmas cookie cutters
Coloured icing
Sprinkles or other candy to decorate with

This is one Christmas activity that my sisters and I looked forward to all year. Make up a batch of *Cookie Cut-outs* (Chapter 4), sugar cookies, or other rolled dough cookies. Use Christmas cookie cutters to cut out angels, Christmas trees, bells, etc. When baked and cooled, set your child up at the table with the cookies, bowls of icing in various colours, and all kinds of little goodies for decorating: sprinkles, raisins, chocolate chips, gumdrops, etc. She will probably eat more than she decorates, but this will become a well-cherished memory.

Christmas Tree Picture (#350)

Construction paper in green and other colours
Hole punch
Glue
Sequins or glitter

Cut out a Christmas tree from green construction paper. Use a paper hole punch to punch out coloured dots from construction paper. Glue the dots to your tree for decorations; add sequins or glitter and a star at the top.

Glitter Snowflakes (#351)

Wax paper
White glue
Glitter
Thread

Drip glue in a snowflake design onto the wax side of a piece of wax paper. Have your child sprinkle glitter on top of the glue and allow to dry for one or two days. Peel the snowflake off the wax paper carefully, and tie thread around one point. Hang it in a window or doorway, or tape to your child's bedroom door.

Thank You Cards (#352)

Construction or plain paper
Markers or crayons
Stickers (optional)
Cookie cutters (optional)
Old Christmas cards (optional)
Scissors (optional)
Glue (optional)

Making thank you cards in advance is one way of making sure they are sent out promptly when gifts are received. Fold a sheet of paper in half or quarters and decorate with crayons or markers, or try some of these ideas:
- decorate with Christmas stickers;
- trace around Christmas cookie cutters;
- trace around your child's hand;
- cut up old Christmas cards and glue on;
- colour sideways over a card with a raised design
  (see *Christmas Rubbings*).

Christmas Chain (#353)

Construction paper in red and green
Glue or paste

Cut strips of red and green construction paper, three to four inches long and one-half to one inch wide. Form a circle with one strip, gluing the ends together. Take the next strip and loop it through the first circle, again gluing the ends together. Continue on and make a chain as long as you want. Use to decorate the Christmas tree, doorways, walls, etc.

Christmas Rubbings (#354)

Christmas card with a raised picture
Plain white paper
Crayons

Lay a piece of white paper over a Christmas card with a raised picture on it. Your child can rub a crayon sideways over the paper and watch the design appear.

Reindeer Antlers (#355)

Brown construction paper
Glue

Using brown construction paper, cut a band to fit your child's head. Trace her handprints on the paper, cut out and glue to the headband as reindeer antlers.

Christmas Wish List (#356)

Old Christmas catalog or magazines
Construction paper or light cardboard
Glue or paste
Clear contact paper

Have your child cut out her wishes from a catalog and glue them onto a piece of construction paper. Cover with clear contact paper and use as a placemat.

Rice Krispie Snowman or Christmas Tree (#357)

5 cups Rice Krispies
1/4 cup margarine or butter
4 cups miniature marshmallows or 40 regular marshmallows
10 to 12 regular marshmallows
Toothpicks
Green food colouring (for tree)
Red cinnamon candies (for tree)
Shredded coconut (for snowman)
Candy for decoration (for snowman)

Melt margarine in a 3-quart saucepan, then add miniature marshmallows and cook over low heat, stirring constantly, until syrupy. Remove from heat. If making a Christmas tree, add green food colouring until a fairly dark green colour. Add Rice Krispies and stir until well coated.

To make a Christmas tree, shape into conical forms with buttered hands. When cooled, stick a toothpick through a marshmallow and stick into the bottom to serve as the tree's base. Decorate with red candies.

To make a snowman, shape into a small, medium and large ball and roll in coconut "snow". Use toothpicks to join the balls to form the snowman. Decorate with various candies.

Snow Globe (#358)

Small baby food jar with lid
Gold or silver glitter
Glue gun
1/4" ribbon
Small toys or ornaments that fit into the jar
Water

Using the hot glue gun, glue ornaments or small toys to the inside of the lid of the jar and allow to dry. Have your child fill the jar with water and add glitter. Place the lid on the jar tightly and glue the ribbon over the edge of the lid to seal. Show your child how to shake up a snowstorm inside the jar.

Paper Plate Snowman (#359)

Cardboard or three small paper plates
Felt scraps
Glue
Paint or markers
Stapler
Scissors

Cut three circles of increasing size from paper plates or cardboard. Staple the circles together; one plate is the snowman's head and two make his body. Glue cotton balls on if you like. Cut his scarf, buttons, features and hat out of felt and glue on. If you don't use cotton balls, paint the face with paint or markers, then glue on his accessories.

Christmas Card Puzzles (#360)

Christmas cards you have received
Heavy paper or cardboard
Glue
Scissors

Glue Christmas cards onto heavy paper or cardboard. When dry, cut into puzzles.

Christmas Bells (#361)

Egg carton
Scissors
Jingle bells
Yarn, string or ribbon
Glue (optional)
Glitter (optional)
Paint (optional)
Aluminum foil (optional)

Cut an egg carton into individual sections; paint or decorate with glitter, or cover with a small square of aluminum foil. Make a small hole in the top of each egg cup. Cut yarn or string into 6" lengths and poke one end through the hole in the top of the egg cup. Thread the bottom piece of string through a jingle bell and back up through the hole at the top of the cup. Knot the ends. Hang on doorknobs (you may need a longer length of string) or as Christmas tree ornaments.

Paper Plate Wreath (#362)

Green paper plate
Red and green tissue paper
Ribbon bow
Scissors
Glue

Cut a hole in the centre of the plate to make the shape of the wreath. Cut or tear red and green tissue paper into small pieces. Twist the paper or crumple into small balls and glue onto the plate. Add a ribbon bow in a contrasting colour.

Christmas Card Holder (#363)

Large green poster board
Small yellow poster board
Large coloured clothespins or plastic paper clips
Glue
Heavy tape
Ribbon
Hole puncher
Scissors

Cut a green triangle and a yellow star out of poster board. Glue the star to the top of the green triangle. Glue paper clips or clothespins onto the green triangle Christmas tree. When dry, punch a hole through the poster board where the tree and star meet. Loop a ribbon through the hole and tie a knot. Hang on a hook on the wall, or use heavy tape to attach to the fridge or your child's bedroom door. (Try adapting this idea for other occasions: make a Valentine holder by gluing clips onto a big heart cut from red posterboard, or cut out a large number "4" and glue on clips to hold cards from your child's fourth birthday.)

Lollipop Tree (#364)

> Bag of lollipops
> Styrofoam cone
> Scissors

Divide a bag of lollipops into three groups; one group will be used for the bottom of the tree, one for the middle, and one for the top. Set aside one group for the bottom; cut the sticks of one of the remaining groups short for the top of the tree, the other group medium for the middle. Show your child how to poke the lollipops into a small styrofoam cone to make a lollipop tree.

Candy Advent Calendar (#365)

> Red or green poster board (or construction paper glued to a file
>   folder or piece of cardboard)
> Pen or marker
> Old Christmas cards, rubber stamps or Christmas stickers for decorating
> Scissors (optional)
> Glue (optional)
> 25 pieces of wrapped Christmas candy
> *Ornamental Frosting* (see Chapter 2)
> Hole puncher
> Ribbon

Help your child track the number of days until Christmas by making this Candy Advent Calendar with her. Draw a December calendar on the bottom half of a piece of red or green poster board, or use red or green construction paper glued to a file folder or piece of cardboard. Have your child cut designs from old Christmas cards and glue to the top half of the poster board, or decorate with rubber stamps or Christmas stickers. Use *Ornamental Frosting* to stick a small piece of wrapped candy onto each grid of the calendar from December 1st up to December 25th. Lay the calendar flat until the icing has set, then punch a hole in the top and tie on a piece of ribbon for hanging. Each day your child will have a visual and tasty reminder of the number of days until Christmas.

Appendices

"The commonest fallacy among women is that simply having children makes one a mother -- which is as absurd as believing that having a piano makes one a musician."

Sydney J. Harris

Appendix A
Crazy Can Activities

The following activities are suitable for a Crazy Can (see Chapter 1). These activities are suggested because they require no special materials, need no time-consuming preparation or clean-up, and above all, demand a minimal amount of adult participation. Some of these ideas do require a little advance planning (i.e. have a map or clues prepared in advance for the *Indoor Treasure Hunt*). These activities will provide you with an instant remedy when things start to get crazy, or when there's just "nothing to do". (The number following each activity refers to the page number on which that activity is found.)

Appendix B
Best Books for Young Children

The following books are suggested for children up to age 8, either for reading by the child or for reading to him. This list has been compiled from several sources. *Timeless Classics,* published by the National Endowment for the Humanities, is a compilation of tried-and-true titles. These are books published in 1960 or before that have been the favourite of at least one previous generation. Another source is *Reading for the Love of It* by Michele Landsberg (1987, Prentice Hall Press/A division of Simon & Schuster, New York; reprinted by permission of the publisher), an excellent guide to the best books for children of all ages. A final source is the bookshelves in my own children's rooms, favourite volumes that have been read over and over and over again.

Aardema, Verna
  The Vingananee and the Tree Toad
  Why Mosquitoes Buzz in People's Ears

Aesop
  Aesop's Fables

Alderson, Sue Ann
  Bonnie McSmithers You're Driving Me Dithers

Allen, Jeffrey
  Mary Alice, Operator Number Nine

Ahlberg, Janet and Allen
  Each Peach Pear Plum

Atwater, Richard and Florence
  Mr. Popper's Penguins

Bemelmans, Ludwig
  Madeline series

Brooke, Leslie L.
  Johnny Crow's Party

Brown, Margaret Wise
  Goodnight Moon

Brunhoff, Jean de
  The Story of Babar

Burninghame, John
  Cannonball Simp
  Harquin, the Fox Who Went Down to the Valley
  Would You Rather?

Burton, Virginia Lee
  Mike Mulligan and His Steam Shovel

Caldicott, Randolph
Hey Diddle Diddle

Clifton, Lucille
Don't You Remember?

Crowther, Robert
The Most Amazing Hide-and-Seek Alphabet Book

Dalgleish, Alice
The Bears on Hemlock Mountain
The Courage of Sarah Noble

Eastman, P.D.
Are You My Mother?
Go, Dog, Go

Flack, Marjorie
The Story about Ping

Freeman, Don
Corduroy

Gag, Wanda
Millions of Cats

Godden, Rumer
The Mousewife

Goffstein, M.B.
Our Snowman

Grahame, Kenneth
The Reluctant Dragon

Haywood, Carolyn
Betsy series

Hoban, Russell
Bread and Jam for Frances

Hutchins, Pat
Rosie's Walk

Jonas, Ann
The Trek

Keats, Ezra Jack
Goggles!

Kellogg, Steven
The Island of the Skog

Kipling, Rudyard
Just So Stories for Little Children

Kovalski, Maryann
Brenda and Edward

Krause, Robert
Herman the Helper
Whose Mouse Are You?

Leaf, Munro
The Story of Ferdinand

Lear, Edward
The Book of Nonsense

MacDonald, Betty
Mrs. Piggle-Wiggle

Marshall, James
George and Martha

McCloskey, Robert
Blueberries for Sal
Make Way for Ducklings

McDermott, Gerald
Papagayo, the Mischeif-maker

Meyer, Mercer
Little Critter series

Milne, A.A.
The House at Pooh Corner
Now We Are Six

When We Were Very Young
Winnie-the-Pooh

Minaruk, Else Holmelund
Little Bear

Mosel, Arlene
The Funny Little Woman
Tikkie Tikki Tembo

Munsch, Robert
I Have To Go
Love You Forever
The Paperbag Princess

Nicoll, Helen
Meg and Mog

Ormerod, Jan
Moonlight
Sunshine

Perrault, Charles
Cinderella

Pinkwater, Manus
Three Big Hogs

Potter, Beatrix
The Tale of Peter Rabbit

Rey, H.A.
Curious George series

Segal, Lore
Tell Me a Mitzi
Tell Me a Trudy

Selden, George
The Cricket in Times Square

Sendak, Maurice
Where the Wild Things Are

Seuss, Dr.
Green Eggs and Ham
The Cat in the Hat
The 500 Hats of Bartholomew Cubbin

Shulevitz, Uri
One Monday Morning

Steig, William
Brave Irene
Sylvester and the Magic Pebble

Stevenson, James
Could Be Worse!

Stevenson, John
Clams Can't Sing

Stevenson, Robert Louis
A Child's Garden of Verses

Stamm, Claus
Three Strong Women

Viorst, Judith
Alexander and the Terrible, Horrible,
No Good, Very Bad Day

Waber, Bernard
Lyle the Crocodile series

Wagner, Jenny
The Bunyip of Berkeley's Creek

Wallace, Ian
Chin Chiang and the Dragon's Dance

Watson, Clyde
Applebet, an ABC

Wells, Rosemary
Noisy Nora

Wildsmith, Brian
Cat on the Mat

Appendix C
Gifts for Kids to Make and Give

Most kids love to give gifts almost as much as they love to receive them, and the excitement is usually intensified if the gift is something they have made themselves. The following activities provide fun and easy ways for kids to personalize their gift-giving. The number following each activity refers to the page number on which that activity is found.

The following activities can be used to create unique and personal greetings cards and giftwrap.

Appendix D - Resources

This book is a combination of personal experience, contributions from friends and family, and ideas and information gathered from the books and government publications listed below.

Baby Games, Elaine Martin, Stoddart Publishing, 1988

Becoming a Nation of Readers: What Parents Can Do, D.C. Heath and Company and the U.S. Department of Education, 1988

Children's Art & Crafts, Nancy Lewis Bartlctt, The Australian Women's Weekly Home Library, Australian Consolidated Press, 1991

Creative Family Times, Allen & Connie Hadidian, Will & Lindy Wilson, Moody Press, 1989

Dance and Your Child, The National Dance Association and The National Endowment for the Arts, 1991

Feed Me! I'm Yours, Vicky Lansky, Meadowbrook Press, 1974

From Words to Stories, Teachers and Writers Collaborative and The National Endowment for the Arts, 1991

Help! I Have a Pre-school Child!!!, Kandi Arnold, Andrea Devin, Dale Sprowl, Garborg's Heart 'N Home, 1990

Help Your Child Become a Good Reader, U.S. Department of Education

Helping Your Child Learn Geography, U.S. Department of Education, 1990

Lollipop Grapes & Clothespin Critters, Robyn Freedman Spitzman, Addison-Wesley Publishing, 1985

Mother's Almanac, The, Marguerite Kelly & Elia Parsons, Doubleday, 1975

Mother's Manual for Summer Survival, A, Kathy Peel & Joy Mahaffey, Focus on the Family Publishing, 1989

Music and Your Child's Education, The Music Educators National Conference and The National Endowment for the Arts, 1991

Papier Mâché Artistry, Dona Z. Meilach, General Publishing, 1971

Prime Time Together ... With Kids, Donna Erickson, Augsburg Fortress, 1989

Rainy Day Activities for Preschoolers, Ann Marie Connolly & Helen Gibson, Mercer Island Preschool Association,

1988

Reading for the Love of It, Michele Landsberg, Prentice Hall Press, 1987

Sunset Children's Crafts, Lane Publishing Co., 1976

Theater and Children, American Alliance for Theatre & Education and The National Endowment for the Arts, 1991

Timeless Classics, National Endowment for the Humanities, 1991

What To Do After You Turn Off The TV, Frances Moore Lappé, Random House, 1985

You Can Help Your Young Child Learn Mathematics, U.S. Department of Education, 1991

Your Baby & Child From Birth to Age Five, Penelope Leach, Random House, 1989

Your Child and the Visual Arts, The National Art Education Association and The National Endowment for the Arts, 1991

The United States General Services Administration makes available many free and low-cost federal publications of consumer interest, including many on *Learning Activities* and *Parenting*. For a free catalog write to:

Consumer Information Centre-2C
P.O. Box 100
Pueblo, Colorado 81002

Index

"When you are dealing with a child, keep all your wits about you, and sit on the floor."

Austin O'Malley

About the Author

Patricia Kuffner lives with her husband and three children on an acreage in Coquitlam, just outside of Vancouver, B.C. After the birth of their second child, Trish left a demanding computer programming position to join the growing number of women choosing full-time motherhood over career. This is her first book.

Canadian readers:

Use this convenient order form to order additional copies of
Surviving Your Preschooler ... A Mother's Manual.

Surviving Your Preschooler ... A Mother's Manual makes a wonderful gift for family and friends with young children. This book is available in many fine book stores across the country. We appreciate the support these stores have given us and encourage you to patronize them. But if your local stores aren't carrying it, we'd be happy to fill your mail order. Just complete the form below.

Special discounts are available to those who purchase in bulk, making *Surviving Your Preschooler ... A Mother's Manual* a natural fundraiser for preschools, daycares, churches and playgroups. For quantity discount information, write to us at the address below.

• •

Canadian Order Form

**Number
of Copies**

Total

Surviving Your Preschooler ... A
Mother's Manual, at $16.95/each

_____   _____

Postage and Handling ($2.50 per book)   _____

                                                   Subtotal   _____

GST (7% of subtotal)   _____

                                          Total Enclosed   _____

Please make your cheque or money order payable in Canadian funds to:
Lighthouse Books, 1423 Dayton Street, Coquitlam, B.C., V3P 1B3
Phone/Fax (604) 945-0266

Send books to: *(please print)*

Name _____

Address _____

City _____

Province _____ Postal Code _____

Thank you for your order!

U.S. customers - please use order form on reverse.

Use this convenient order form to order additional copies of *Surviving Your Preschooler ... A Mother's Manual.*

Surviving Your Preschooler ... A Mother's Manual makes a wonderful gift for family and friends with young children. This book is presently available in the U.S. only through mail order. To order additional copies, just complete the form below.

Special discounts are available to those who purchase in bulk, making *Surviving Your Preschooler ... A Mother's Manual* a natural fundraiser for preschools, daycares, churches and playgroups. For quantity discount information, write to us at the address below.

• •

U.S. Order Form

Number of Copies　　　　　　　　　　　　　　　　　　　　　　　　　　**Total**

_____　Surviving Your Preschooler ... A
　　　　　　　　　Mother's Manual, at $12.95/each　**Subtotal**　_____

　　　　　　　　　Postage and Handling ($3.00 per book)　_____

　　　　　　　　　　　　　　　　　　　Total Enclosed　_____

Please make your check or money order payable in U.S. funds to:
Lighthouse Books, 1733 H Street, Suite #330-524, Blaine, WA 98230
Phone/Fax (604) 945-0266

Send books to: *(please print)*

Name　_____

Address　_____

City　_____

State　_____ Zip Code　_____

Thank you for your order!

Canadian customers - please use order form on reverse.